Taste of Tradition

Classic Recipes with a Modern Twist

MAISIE LITTLE

The presentation of the information is without contract or any type of guarantee assurance. The trademarks that are used are without any consent, and the publication of the trademark is without permission or backing by the trademark owner. All trademarks and brands within this book are for clarifying purposes only and are the owned by the owners themselves, not affiliated with this document.

Table of Contents

Chapter 1

Introduction: The Fusion of Past and Present

The Essence of Traditional Cooking

Traditional cooking is more than just a method of preparing food; it is a tapestry woven with history, culture, and family traditions. Its essence lies not only in the ingredients and techniques but also in the stories and emotions that come with each dish. From the bustling markets of Marrakech to the quiet kitchens of rural Italy, traditional cooking forms the backbone of culinary heritage worldwide.

To understand traditional cooking, one must first appreciate the significance of local ingredients. In many cultures, the availability of ingredients defines the cuisine. For example, the Mediterranean diet is rich in olives, tomatoes, and seafood, all of which are abundant in the region. Similarly, the spices used in Indian cuisine, such as turmeric, cumin, and coriander, are native to the subcontinent and have been used for centuries. The reliance on local produce not only ensures freshness but also fosters a deep connection between the people and their land.

The methods used in traditional cooking are often labor-intensive and time-consuming, reflecting the care and attention given to each dish. Techniques such as fermentation, smoking, and slow-cooking are common across many cultures. Fermentation, for instance, is a method used globally, from kimchi in Korea to sauerkraut in Germany. This process not only preserves food but also enhances its nutritional value and flavor. Smoking, another ancient technique, is used in various forms, whether it's the smoked salmon of Scandinavia or the barbecued meats of the American South. These methods require patience and skill, qualities that are integral to traditional cooking.

Recipes in traditional cooking are often passed down through generations, with each family adding its own unique touch. These recipes are more than just instructions; they are heirlooms that carry memories and stories. In many cultures, cooking is a communal activity, bringing families and communities together. For example, the Italian tradition of making pasta by hand is often a family affair, with grandparents teaching their grandchildren the art of rolling and cutting dough. Similarly, in Mexico, the preparation of tamales is a social event, with family members gathering to make large batches for special occasions. These traditions foster a sense of belonging and continuity.

Traditional cooking also emphasizes the importance of seasonal eating. Before the advent of modern preservation methods, people relied on what was available at different times of the year. This practice not only ensured a varied diet but also respected the natural cycles of the earth. For example, in Japan, the concept of "shun" refers to the time of year when a particular ingredient is at its peak flavor and nutritional value. This principle guides Japanese cuisine, where dishes are designed to highlight the season's best produce. Similarly, in Europe, the harvest season is celebrated with festivals and feasts, showcasing the bounty of the land.

The tools and equipment used in traditional cooking are often simple but effective. Clay pots, wooden spoons, and stone grinders are common in many kitchens around the world. These tools, often handmade, are designed to enhance the cooking process. For example, the Moroccan tagine, a clay pot with a conical lid, is perfect for slow-cooking stews, allowing the flavors to meld together beautifully. In India, the use of a tandoor, a clay oven, imparts a unique smoky flavor to breads and meats. These traditional tools are not only functional but also hold cultural significance, often being passed down through families as treasured possessions.

The role of traditional cooking in health and wellness cannot be overstated. Many traditional diets are inherently balanced and nutritious, emphasizing whole foods and natural ingredients. For example, the Mediterranean diet, rich in fruits, vegetables, whole grains, and healthy fats, is renowned for its health benefits, including reduced risks of heart disease and longevity. Similarly, the traditional Japanese diet, with its emphasis on fish, rice, and vegetables, is associated with some of the highest life expectancies in the world. These diets, developed over centuries, reflect a deep understanding of nutrition and well-being.

In many cultures, traditional cooking is intertwined with rituals and celebrations. Food plays a central role in festivals, religious ceremonies, and life events. For example, in China, the Lunar New Year is celebrated with an array of symbolic dishes, each representing prosperity, luck, and happiness. In India, the festival of Diwali is marked by the preparation of sweets and savory snacks, shared with family and friends. These culinary traditions are not just about eating but are expressions of cultural identity and values.

The preservation of traditional cooking methods is vital in an age of globalization and fast food. As the world becomes increasingly homogenized, there is a risk of losing these rich culinary traditions. Efforts to document and teach traditional cooking are crucial for keeping these practices alive. Culinary schools, food historians, and cultural organizations play a significant role in this endeavor. For example, the Slow Food movement, founded in Italy, advocates for the preservation of traditional and regional cuisine, emphasizing the importance of local food cultures.

Incorporating traditional cooking into modern life can be challenging but rewarding. It requires a shift in mindset, valuing quality and authenticity over convenience. For those seeking to explore traditional cooking, starting with a single dish or technique can be a manageable approach. For example, learning to bake bread from scratch can be a fulfilling experience, connecting you to a practice that dates back thousands of years. Similarly, growing your own herbs or vegetables can provide a deeper appreciation for the ingredients you use.

In conclusion, the essence of traditional cooking lies in its deep roots in history, culture, and community. It is a reflection of the land and its people, passed down through generations with love and care. By embracing traditional cooking, we not only preserve these rich culinary heritages but also enrich our own lives, fostering a deeper connection to our food and the stories it tells. The essence of traditional cooking also shines through in the relationship between food and the environment. Many traditional practices emphasize sustainability and respect for nature, long before these concepts became modern-day buzzwords. Indigenous cuisines, for example, often demonstrate a profound understanding of ecological balance. The Native American "Three Sisters" planting method, which involves growing corn, beans, and squash together, exemplifies this harmony. Corn provides a structure for the beans to climb, beans restore nitrogen to the soil, and squash spreads out to prevent weeds. Such practices show an intrinsic respect for the land and a recognition of the interconnectedness of all living things.

The Art of Modern Culinary Innovation

Modern culinary innovation is a fascinating blend of creativity, science, and tradition. It is a dynamic field where chefs and food enthusiasts continually push the boundaries of what is possible in the kitchen. This chapter delves into the essence of culinary innovation, exploring how contemporary chefs integrate new techniques, ingredients, and philosophies to create dishes that astonish and delight the senses.

Culinary innovation often begins with a re-examination of traditional methods and recipes. Chefs look to the past for inspiration, understanding the historical context of classic dishes before reimagining them for a modern audience. This involves not only a deep respect for tradition but also a willingness to experiment and adapt. For example, Ferran Adrià, the renowned Spanish chef, revolutionized the culinary world with his avant-garde approach at El Bulli. By deconstructing traditional Spanish cuisine and employing techniques such as spherification and foam creation, Adrià transformed familiar flavors into entirely new experiences. His work exemplifies how modern culinary innovation can honor tradition while boldly venturing into uncharted territories.

A key aspect of modern culinary innovation is the incorporation of scientific principles into cooking. Molecular gastronomy, a term popularized by French chemist Hervé This, explores the physical and chemical transformations that occur during cooking. This scientific approach allows chefs to manipulate textures and flavors in ways previously thought impossible. For instance, the use of liquid nitrogen to create ultra-smooth ice creams or the application of hydrocolloids to alter the viscosity of sauces are techniques born from this marriage of science and culinary art. These innovations not only enhance the sensory experience of food but also expand the possibilities for creative expression in the kitchen.

Another driving force behind modern culinary innovation is the quest for sustainability. As awareness of environmental issues grows, chefs are increasingly focused on creating dishes that are not only delicious but also sustainable. This involves sourcing ingredients responsibly, reducing waste, and considering the environmental impact of culinary practices. René Redzepi, the chef behind Noma in Copenhagen, is a pioneer in this field. His commitment to foraging and using local, seasonal ingredients has not only redefined Nordic cuisine but also set a global standard for sustainable dining. By embracing sustainability, modern culinary innovators demonstrate that creativity and responsibility can go hand in hand.

The integration of technology into the kitchen has also played a significant role in modern culinary innovation. Advanced cooking equipment, such as sous-vide machines and combi ovens, allows for precise control over cooking processes. Sous-vide, for example, involves vacuum-sealing food and cooking it at a low, consistent temperature in a water bath. This method ensures even cooking and enhances the natural flavors of the ingredients. Similarly, combi ovens, which combine convection and steam cooking, offer versatility and precision, enabling chefs to achieve perfect results with a variety of dishes. These technologies provide chefs with new tools to refine their craft and push the boundaries of culinary creativity.

In addition to technological advancements, modern culinary innovation is also driven by the exploration of new ingredients. Chefs are continually seeking out unique and exotic ingredients to incorporate into their dishes. This curiosity has led to the discovery and popularization of ingredients such as yuzu, a citrus fruit from Japan, and teff, an ancient grain from Ethiopia. By experimenting with these ingredients, chefs introduce diners to new flavors and textures, broadening their culinary horizons. The willingness to explore and experiment with new ingredients is a hallmark of modern culinary innovation, reflecting a globalized world where cultural exchanges enrich the culinary landscape.

The art of plating and presentation has also evolved significantly in the realm of modern culinary innovation. Contemporary chefs view the plate as a canvas, where the visual appeal of a dish is as important as its taste. Techniques such as micro-greens, edible flowers, and intricate garnishes are used to create visually stunning dishes that captivate diners before they even take a bite. The rise of social media platforms like Instagram has further amplified the importance of food presentation, as visually striking dishes are more likely to be shared and celebrated online. This emphasis on aesthetics challenges chefs to think creatively about how they present their food, making each dish a feast for the eyes as well as the palate.

Collaboration and cross-disciplinary influences are also central to modern culinary innovation. Chefs often collaborate with artists, designers, and scientists to create unique dining experiences. For instance, the collaboration between chef Heston Blumenthal and perfumer Roja Dove resulted in the creation of a dish that engaged all five senses, using scent to enhance the dining experience. Such partnerships bring fresh perspectives and ideas into the culinary world, leading to the creation of dishes that are truly innovative and multi-dimensional.

Modern culinary innovation is not confined to high-end restaurants and professional kitchens. Home cooks, too, are embracing innovative techniques and ingredients, thanks in part to the accessibility of information and tools. Cookbooks, online tutorials, and cooking shows provide valuable resources for those looking to experiment in their own kitchens. The rise of food blogs and social media has also created a community of enthusiastic home cooks who share their creations and inspire others to try new things. This democratization of culinary innovation means that anyone with a passion for cooking can explore and contribute to the ever-evolving world of food.

One of the most exciting aspects of modern culinary innovation is its potential to create memorable dining experiences. Chefs are increasingly focusing on the experiential aspect of dining, designing meals that engage all the senses and tell a story. The concept of a tasting menu, where diners are taken on a culinary journey through a series of small, carefully crafted dishes, exemplifies this approach. Each course is designed to build on the previous one, creating a cohesive and immersive experience. By paying attention to details such as lighting, music, and even the texture of the tableware, chefs create an environment where the act of dining becomes a form of art.

In conclusion, the art of modern culinary innovation is a dynamic and multifaceted field that blends tradition, science, sustainability, technology, and creativity. It challenges chefs and home cooks alike to think beyond conventional boundaries and explore new possibilities. By embracing innovation, we not only enhance our culinary experiences but also contribute to a rich and diverse food culture that continues to evolve and inspire. The journey of culinary innovation is one of discovery and transformation, where each dish tells a story and every meal is an opportunity to create something extraordinary. This dynamic interplay of elements ensures that the culinary world remains vibrant and ever-evolving. As we continue to explore the art of modern culinary innovation, it becomes evident that the journey is as important as the destination. Each experiment, each new technique, and each novel ingredient contributes to a broader understanding of what food can be.

Why Blend Tradition with Modernity?

Balancing tradition with modernity in contemporary culinary arts is akin to walking a tightrope. It requires skill, vision, and an appreciation for both the past and the future. This delicate balance is not merely a trend, but a crucial aspect of innovation that honors heritage while embracing progress. Understanding why it is essential to blend tradition with modernity is key to mastering the art of cooking in today's world.

Tradition provides a foundation of time-tested techniques, flavors, and recipes that have been honed over generations. These elements are the bedrock of culinary arts, offering a rich tapestry of cultural and historical contexts. For instance, consider the Italian tradition of pasta making. This technique, passed down through countless generations, ensures that the texture, flavor, and quality of the pasta remain unparalleled. When a modern chef takes this traditional method and introduces new ingredients or presentation styles, the dish evolves while still retaining its authentic roots.

Incorporating modern elements into traditional dishes allows for creative expression and innovation. It is through this fusion that chefs can push the boundaries of culinary arts, creating dishes that are both familiar and exciting. For example, modern techniques such as sous-vide cooking or molecular gastronomy can enhance traditional recipes, offering new textures and flavor profiles while maintaining the essence of the original dish. This approach not only respects the past but also acknowledges the advancements in culinary science and technology.

Another reason to blend tradition with modernity is the dynamic nature of food culture. As societies evolve, so do their culinary preferences and dietary needs. Traditional dishes must adapt to contemporary tastes and nutritional requirements to remain relevant. This adaptation can be seen in the growing trend of plant-based diets. Traditional recipes are being reimagined to include plant-based ingredients, catering to a more health-conscious and environmentally aware audience. For instance, the classic American burger has been transformed by using plant-based patties, offering a modern twist on a beloved staple while addressing current dietary trends.

The fusion of tradition and modernity also fosters cultural exchange and understanding. In today's globalized world, culinary arts serve as a bridge between different cultures. By blending traditional elements from various cuisines with modern techniques, chefs can create dishes that celebrate diversity and promote cross-cultural appreciation. Consider the popularity of fusion cuisine, which combines elements from different culinary traditions to create something entirely new. Dishes like sushi burritos or kimchi tacos exemplify this blend, showcasing how traditional flavors can be reinterpreted through a modern lens, resulting in innovative and globally inspired creations.

Moreover, blending tradition with modernity can enhance the dining experience, making it more engaging and memorable. Modern presentation techniques, such as dramatic plating and interactive dining experiences, can elevate traditional dishes, creating a sense of excitement and wonder for diners. Imagine a traditional French dish like coq au vin, served in a deconstructed form with each element artfully presented on the plate. This modern interpretation not only highlights the skill and creativity of the chef but also invites diners to experience the dish in a new and captivating way.

Sustainability is another critical factor driving the fusion of tradition and modernity. As the culinary world grapples with issues like food waste, resource scarcity, and environmental impact, chefs are turning to traditional practices that emphasize sustainability. Techniques such as fermentation, pickling, and nose-to-tail cooking are being revived and integrated with modern approaches to create sustainable culinary practices. For example, traditional methods of preserving food through fermentation are being combined with modern scientific understanding to develop new, probiotic-rich dishes that are both healthful and environmentally friendly.

Blending tradition with modernity also allows chefs to tell a story through their food. Every dish becomes a narrative, weaving together elements of history, culture, and personal creativity. This storytelling aspect adds depth and meaning to the dining experience, forging a connection between the chef and the diner. A dish that combines traditional ingredients and methods from a chef's heritage with modern techniques and presentation can convey a powerful message about identity, heritage, and innovation. This narrative approach not only enriches the dining experience but also preserves cultural heritage while pushing the boundaries of culinary arts.

From a practical standpoint, blending tradition with modernity can also be a strategic business move for restaurants and food businesses. It allows them to appeal to a broader audience, attracting both traditionalists who appreciate classic flavors and adventurous diners seeking new experiences. This dual appeal can enhance a restaurant's reputation and broaden its customer base, ensuring its relevance and success in a competitive market. Additionally, offering a menu that incorporates both traditional and modern elements can set a restaurant apart, making it a destination for diners who crave a unique and memorable experience.

Education and mentorship play a vital role in this fusion. Aspiring chefs and culinary students benefit from learning both traditional techniques and modern innovations. This comprehensive education equips them with a versatile skill set, enabling them to create dishes that are rooted in tradition yet forward-thinking. By understanding the historical and cultural significance of traditional methods, young chefs can appreciate the value of these practices while also being encouraged to experiment and innovate. This blend of knowledge and creativity is essential for the future of culinary arts, ensuring that the next generation of chefs is well-prepared to carry the torch of tradition while forging new paths.

In conclusion, blending tradition with modernity in the culinary arts is not just about creating exciting dishes; it is a holistic approach that respects the past, embraces the present, and anticipates the future. It allows chefs to honor their heritage while exploring new frontiers of creativity and innovation. This fusion enhances the dining experience, promotes sustainability, and fosters cultural exchange. By weaving together the threads of tradition and modernity, chefs can create a rich and diverse culinary tapestry that delights the senses and nourishes the soul. This balance is essential for preserving the cultural significance of traditional dishes while ensuring their relevance in a rapidly changing world. Through this harmonious blend, the culinary arts continue to evolve, inspiring both chefs and diners to appreciate the beauty and complexity of food. As we delve deeper into the concept of blending tradition with modernity, it's important to recognize the role of ingredients in this fusion. The sourcing and use of ingredients are fundamental to both traditional and modern cooking. Traditional cuisines often rely on locally sourced, seasonal ingredients, which not only support local economies but also ensure freshness and flavor. Modern culinary practices, on the other hand, benefit from global supply chains and technological advancements that make exotic ingredients more accessible. However, a growing movement within the culinary world emphasizes the importance of reconnecting with local, sustainable sources, blending the best of both worlds.

A Journey through Culinary Heritage

Embarking on a journey through culinary heritage is akin to opening a treasure chest filled with the flavors, aromas, and techniques that have shaped human civilization. Each dish tells a story, connecting us to our ancestors and offering a glimpse into their lives and cultures. Exploring culinary heritage is not just about savoring delicious food; it's about understanding the roots of culinary traditions, appreciating the evolution of ingredients and methods, and preserving these treasures for future generations.

The origins of many culinary traditions can be traced back to ancient civilizations. For instance, the use of spices in cooking dates back thousands of years to the spice routes that connected the East and West. These routes facilitated the exchange of spices like cinnamon, black pepper, and cloves, which were once as valuable as gold. In ancient Egypt, food was a significant part of religious rituals, with bread and beer being staple items. The Greeks and Romans further expanded culinary arts by incorporating a variety of ingredients and techniques, such as the use of olive oil, wine, and honey in their cooking.

As we journey through culinary heritage, we must recognize the impact of geography and climate on food traditions. The ingredients and dishes of a region are often a direct reflection of its natural resources. In coastal areas, seafood becomes a central part of the diet, while in mountainous regions, people rely on hardy crops and livestock. For example, the Mediterranean diet, renowned for its health benefits, is rooted in the abundant availability of fresh vegetables, fruits, fish, and olive oil in the region. Similarly, Scandinavian cuisine features preserved foods like pickled herring and cured meats, reflecting the need to store food for long, harsh winters.

Migration and trade have also played crucial roles in shaping culinary heritage. When people move, they bring their food traditions with them, blending them with local customs and ingredients. This fusion often results in the creation of entirely new culinary traditions. The introduction of tomatoes, potatoes, and chili peppers to Europe after the discovery of the Americas revolutionized European cuisine. Italian cuisine, for instance, is now inseparable from tomatoes, which were unknown in Italy before the 16th century. Similarly, the spices of India have found their way into British cuisine, resulting in dishes like chicken tikka masala, which many consider a British national dish.

Culinary heritage is also deeply intertwined with cultural and religious practices. Festivals, rituals, and celebrations often feature specific foods that hold symbolic meaning. Take, for instance, the Jewish tradition of eating matzo during Passover, symbolizing the haste with which the Israelites left

Egypt, leaving no time for their bread to rise. In India, sweets like laddoos and jalebis are integral to festive celebrations, symbolizing joy and prosperity. Such traditions not only preserve culinary heritage but also reinforce cultural identity and community bonds.

Family recipes are another vital aspect of culinary heritage. Passed down through generations, these recipes are cherished heirlooms that carry the essence of family history and tradition. They are often guarded secrets, with each generation adding its own touch. Cooking these dishes is a way of honoring one's ancestors and keeping their memories alive. For many, the smell and taste of a family recipe can evoke powerful emotions and memories. A grandmother's apple pie or a father's secret barbecue sauce can transcend time, connecting family members across generations.

Preserving culinary heritage in the modern world requires conscious effort and dedication. In an era dominated by fast food and convenience, traditional cooking techniques and recipes are at risk of being forgotten. However, there has been a resurgence of interest in preserving and reviving these traditions. Chefs and home cooks alike are increasingly turning to ancient grains, heirloom vegetables, and traditional methods like fermentation and pickling. This movement is not just about nostalgia; it's about sustainability and health. Traditional diets, often based on whole foods and seasonal ingredients, can offer valuable lessons for contemporary eating habits.

Culinary heritage also offers a rich source of inspiration for modern chefs and food enthusiasts. By studying traditional techniques and recipes, one can gain a deeper understanding of flavor profiles and cooking methods. This knowledge can then be applied in innovative ways to create new dishes that pay homage to the past while embracing contemporary tastes. For example, the practice of nose-to-tail cooking, which uses every part of the animal, is rooted in traditional practices of resourcefulness and respect for food. Modern chefs have revived this approach, creating dishes that are both sustainable and delicious.

Storytelling is a powerful tool in preserving and sharing culinary heritage. Each dish has a story to tell, from its origins and cultural significance to the memories it evokes. By sharing these stories, we can keep culinary traditions alive and pass them on to future generations. Cookbooks, food blogs, and culinary documentaries play a crucial role in this endeavor. They capture the essence of culinary heritage and make it accessible to a wider audience. For instance, the global popularity of Japanese sushi can be attributed not only to its exquisite taste but also to the stories of master sushi chefs and their meticulous craftsmanship.

Education is another vital aspect of preserving culinary heritage. Teaching children and young adults about traditional foods and cooking methods can instill a sense of pride and appreciation for their cultural heritage. Cooking classes, food festivals, and cultural exchanges can provide hands-on experiences that bring culinary traditions to life. Schools and community centers can play an important role by incorporating culinary heritage into their curricula and activities.

In the digital age, technology can also aid in the preservation and promotion of culinary heritage. Digital archives, online recipe collections, and virtual cooking classes can make traditional recipes and techniques accessible to a global audience. Social media platforms allow people to share their culinary creations and stories, fostering a sense of community and cultural exchange. However, it is essential to balance the convenience of technology with the authenticity and hands-on experience of traditional cooking.

In conclusion, a journey through culinary heritage is a journey through time, culture, and memory. It is an exploration of the flavors, techniques, and stories that have shaped our culinary landscape. By preserving and celebrating these traditions, we honor our ancestors and ensure that their legacy continues to inspire and nourish future generations. Culinary heritage is not just about food; it is about identity, community, and the shared human experience. As we savor the tastes of the past, we connect with our roots and embrace the rich tapestry of global culinary traditions. As we delve deeper into the world of culinary heritage, it becomes clear that the preservation of traditional foodways is not merely an act of nostalgia, but a vital practice for maintaining cultural diversity and fostering global understanding. Culinary heritage, with its rich tapestry of flavors and techniques, serves as a bridge between generations, communities, and even nations.

How to Use This Book

Finding a comprehensive guide that seamlessly blends practical advice with engaging storytelling is rare, but that's precisely what this book aims to offer. Whether you're a novice stepping into a new field or someone seeking to deepen your understanding, this book has been crafted to be your companion on this journey.

To get the most out of this book, start by familiarizing yourself with the layout. Each chapter is designed to stand alone, providing in-depth insights into specific topics. This means you can jump to any chapter that catches your interest without worrying about missing crucial information from previous sections. However, reading the book in sequence will give you a more cohesive understanding of the overarching themes.

Think of this book as both a map and a compass. The map lays out the terrain ahead, giving you a clear view of the landscape. Each chapter serves as a waypoint, guiding you through different aspects of the subject matter. Meanwhile, practical examples and actionable advice act as the compass, helping you navigate the complexities you might encounter.

Interactive elements are woven throughout the text to enhance your learning experience. You'll find exercises, reflections, and scenarios that invite you to apply what you've read. These elements are not mere add-ons but are integral to deepening your understanding. When you come across an exercise, take the time to work through it thoughtfully. This active engagement will solidify your grasp of the material and make it more relevant to your personal context.

Personal stories and anecdotes are included to illustrate key points and to make the content more relatable. These stories are drawn from a diverse range of experiences and are intended to show how the principles discussed can be applied in real-life situations. Pay attention to these narratives—they are not just entertaining but also serve as practical examples that you can learn from.

One of the strengths of this book is its balance between theory and practice. Theoretical concepts are explained in a clear, straightforward manner, making them accessible even if you're new to the field. These concepts are then tied to practical applications, showing you how to implement them in your own life or work. This dual approach ensures that you not only understand the principles but also know how to use them effectively.

Consider keeping a journal as you progress through the book. Jot down your thoughts, reflections, and any questions that arise. This practice will help you internalize the material and track your learning journey. Revisiting your notes periodically can also reveal how your understanding has evolved over time.

Community and collaboration are important themes in this book. While much of your reading will be a solitary activity, remember that learning is often enhanced through interaction with others. Discussing the content with friends, colleagues, or online communities can provide new perspectives and deepen your understanding. Don't hesitate to share your insights and questions—these discussions can lead to valuable exchanges of ideas.

Each chapter concludes with a summary and key takeaways. These sections are designed to reinforce the main points and provide a quick reference for future use. After finishing a chapter, spend a few moments reviewing these summaries. This practice will help consolidate your learning and make it easier to recall the information later.

Flexibility is built into the structure of this book. While it offers a comprehensive guide, it also recognizes that everyone's learning journey is unique. Feel free to adapt the advice and strategies to fit your own needs and circumstances. The goal is not to follow a rigid path but to find the approach that works best for you.

Engaging with additional resources can also enhance your learning experience. Throughout the book, you'll find references to further reading, tools, and other materials that can provide deeper insights into specific topics. Exploring these resources can broaden your understanding and offer new avenues for exploration.

As you work through the book, set aside regular time for reflection. Consider how the material applies to your own experiences and how you can integrate the principles into your daily life. This reflective practice will make the content more meaningful and help you see the practical benefits of what you're learning.

The language used in this book is intentionally clear and accessible. Complex ideas are broken down into manageable pieces, ensuring that you can grasp the concepts without feeling overwhelmed. If you encounter a term or concept that's unfamiliar, take a moment to look it up or refer to the glossary if one is provided. Building a solid foundation of understanding will make it easier to tackle more advanced topics as you progress.

Visual aids such as diagrams, charts, and illustrations are included to complement the text. These aids are designed to clarify complex ideas and provide a visual representation of key concepts. Don't skip over these visuals—they often contain essential information and can make difficult ideas easier to understand.

Feedback is a valuable tool for growth, and this book encourages you to seek it out. Whether you're applying the principles in your personal life or professional setting, asking for feedback from others can provide new insights and help you refine your approach. Be open to constructive criticism and use it as an opportunity to improve.

Finally, remember that learning is a process, not a destination. This book is a guide, but the journey is yours. Embrace the challenges and enjoy the discoveries along the way. The knowledge and skills you gain will be valuable assets, and the effort you invest will pay off in the long run.

By approaching this book with an open mind and a willingness to engage actively with the material, you'll be well on your way to mastering the subject at hand. Whether you're seeking to acquire new skills, deepen your understanding, or simply explore a new area of interest, this book is designed to be a reliable companion on your journey. Your journey through this book is a personal and transformative experience. Each chapter is crafted to build upon the last, creating a cohesive and comprehensive guide that evolves with your understanding. As you delve deeper, you'll find that the principles and practices introduced in earlier chapters lay the foundation for more complex concepts discussed later on. This iterative learning process ensures that you develop a robust and nuanced grasp of the subject matter.

Chapter 2

Breakfast Delights

Classic Pancakes with a Gourmet Twist

A classic pancake, golden brown and fluffy, is a universal comfort food that transcends cultures and breakfast tables alike. However, transforming this humble dish into a gourmet delight requires a blend of creativity, technique, and a willingness to experiment with flavors and textures. This chapter delves into the art of making classic pancakes while introducing gourmet elements that elevate them to a new level of culinary sophistication.

Begin with the fundamentals. A great pancake starts with a well-balanced batter. The key ingredients include flour, eggs, milk, sugar, baking powder, and a pinch of salt. The flour provides structure, the eggs add richness and help bind the ingredients, the milk ensures a smooth and creamy batter, the sugar adds a touch of sweetness, and the baking powder is essential for that desired fluffiness. The salt, though minimal, enhances the overall flavor by balancing the sweetness.

To prepare the batter, first sift the flour, baking powder, and salt into a large mixing bowl. Sifting not only removes any lumps but also aerates the flour, which contributes to the lightness of the pancakes. In a separate bowl, whisk together the eggs and sugar until the mixture is pale and slightly frothy. This step is crucial as it incorporates air, helping the pancakes rise and become fluffy. Gradually add the milk to the egg mixture, whisking continuously to ensure a smooth consistency.

Next, create a well in the center of the dry ingredients and pour in the wet mixture. Using a spatula, gently fold the ingredients together. Be careful not to overmix; a few lumps in the batter are perfectly fine and will result in tender pancakes. Overmixing can lead to tough, dense pancakes, which is the opposite of what we aim to achieve.

Now, let's introduce the gourmet twist. One of the simplest yet most effective ways to elevate pancakes is by infusing the batter with unique flavors. For instance, adding a teaspoon of vanilla extract or a pinch of cinnamon can transform the aroma and taste of the pancakes. For a more decadent twist, consider folding in some finely grated lemon zest and poppy seeds. The zest adds a refreshing citrus note, while the poppy seeds offer a subtle crunch that contrasts beautifully with the soft texture of the pancakes.

Another sophisticated addition is the incorporation of ricotta cheese into the batter. Ricotta pancakes are renowned for their delicate, creamy texture. To achieve this, mix half a cup of ricotta into the wet ingredients before combining them with the dry ingredients. The result is a pancake that is both light and luxurious, with a slight tang from the cheese that pairs wonderfully with sweet toppings.

Speaking of toppings, this is where creativity truly shines. While traditional toppings like maple syrup and butter are timeless, there's a world of gourmet toppings to explore. Consider making a berry compote by simmering fresh or frozen berries with a bit of sugar and lemon juice until they break down into a thick, syrupy sauce. The natural sweetness and acidity of the berries complement the richness of the pancakes perfectly.

For a more indulgent option, try a homemade caramel sauce. Melt sugar in a saucepan until it reaches a deep amber color, then carefully add butter and cream, whisking constantly. The result is a luscious, silky sauce that drapes over the pancakes like a warm, sweet blanket. A sprinkle of sea salt on top of the caramel adds an unexpected but delightful contrast.

For those who enjoy a savory twist, consider topping pancakes with smoked salmon, a dollop of crème fraîche, and a sprinkle of fresh dill. This combination turns a simple breakfast dish into an elegant brunch option, with the smoky, salty salmon balancing the creamy tang of the crème fraîche.

To cook the pancakes, heat a non-stick skillet or griddle over medium heat and lightly grease it with butter or oil. Using a ladle or measuring cup, pour small amounts of batter onto the skillet, forming even circles. Cook until bubbles form on the surface and the edges appear set, then flip and cook until golden brown on the other side. The key is to maintain a consistent temperature to ensure the pancakes cook evenly without burning.

Presentation is another aspect that can elevate your pancakes to gourmet status. Stack the pancakes neatly on a plate and drizzle with your chosen sauce or toppings. A dusting of powdered sugar or a garnish of fresh herbs can add a touch of elegance. When serving, consider pairing the pancakes with complementary sides such as fresh fruit, a light salad, or even a mimosa for a truly luxurious breakfast experience.

Finally, let's talk about variations that cater to different dietary preferences without compromising on the gourmet experience. For gluten-free pancakes, substitute the all-purpose flour with a gluten-free blend. Ensure the blend contains a mix of rice flour, potato starch, and xanthan gum to replicate the texture of traditional pancakes. For a dairy-free version, use almond milk or coconut milk in place of regular milk and substitute the butter with a neutral oil or dairy-free margarine.

Vegan pancakes can be achieved by replacing the eggs with flax or chia seeds mixed with water. This mixture mimics the binding properties of eggs and adds a slight nuttiness to the pancakes. Combine this with a plant-based milk and a good-quality vegan butter, and you'll have pancakes that are just as fluffy and delicious as their traditional counterparts.

In conclusion, making classic pancakes with a gourmet twist involves mastering the basic techniques and then experimenting with flavors, textures, and presentations. By infusing the batter with unique ingredients, exploring a variety of toppings, and paying attention to presentation, you can transform a simple breakfast staple into a sophisticated culinary delight. Whether you're cooking for a special occasion or simply elevating your everyday breakfast, these gourmet pancakes are sure to impress and satisfy. Experimentation is key when striving to elevate your pancakes to gourmet levels. Don't be afraid to try unconventional ingredients that can add complexity and depth to your dish. For instance, incorporating finely chopped nuts, like almonds or pecans, into the batter can introduce a delightful crunch. Alternatively, a handful of dark chocolate chips can melt into gooey pockets of sweetness, creating a decadent treat.

Reinvented Omelets: From Simple to Sophisticated

The omelet, a dish with origins tracing back to ancient Persia, is a staple in kitchens worldwide due to its simplicity and versatility. With just a few eggs and some basic ingredients, you can create a meal that is both satisfying and nutritious. However, the true beauty of an omelet lies in its potential for reinvention. By incorporating a variety of flavors, techniques, and presentations, you can transform a simple omelet into a sophisticated culinary masterpiece.

Begin with the basics. A traditional French omelet, known for its smooth, unbrowned exterior and creamy interior, serves as an excellent foundation. The key to achieving this lies in technique. Start by cracking fresh eggs into a bowl, adding a pinch of salt, and whisking vigorously until the mixture is homogenous and slightly frothy. The vigorous whisking incorporates air, which helps to create a light, fluffy texture.

Heat a non-stick skillet over medium-low heat and add a generous knob of butter. Allow the butter to melt slowly, coating the pan evenly. Pour in the whisked eggs and let them sit undisturbed for a few moments. As the edges begin to set, use a spatula to gently stir the eggs, drawing the cooked portions towards the center. This gentle motion ensures even cooking and prevents the omelet from becoming too dry.

Once the eggs are mostly set but still slightly runny on top, it's time to add the filling. Classic choices include cheese, ham, and fresh herbs, but this is where the opportunity for sophistication arises. Consider incorporating ingredients like sautéed wild mushrooms, caramelized onions, or a medley of fresh herbs such as chives, tarragon, and parsley. These additions not only enhance the flavor but also introduce interesting textures and aromas.

For a touch of luxury, try adding a spoonful of crème fraîche or a sprinkling of truffle oil just before folding the omelet. These ingredients add a rich, creamy element that elevates the dish to gourmet status. Carefully fold one side of the omelet over the filling, slide it onto a plate, and garnish with a few fresh herbs or a light drizzle of olive oil.

Another sophisticated take on the omelet is the Spanish tortilla, a thick, hearty dish traditionally made with potatoes and onions. To make a tortilla, thinly slice potatoes and onions and sauté them in olive oil until tender. In a large bowl, beat the eggs and season with salt and pepper. Add the cooked potatoes and onions to the eggs, stirring to combine.

Heat a non-stick skillet over medium heat and add a bit more olive oil. Pour the egg mixture into the skillet, spreading it out evenly. Cook over low heat until the edges begin to set, then cover the skillet and continue cooking until the top is mostly set but still slightly runny. To finish, place the skillet under a broiler for a few minutes to lightly brown the top. The result is a thick, flavorful omelet that can be served warm or at room temperature, making it perfect for a sophisticated brunch or picnic.

For those seeking a lighter, more delicate option, consider the Japanese tamagoyaki. This omelet is made by layering thin sheets of egg, creating a beautifully rolled and slightly sweet dish. Begin by whisking eggs with a bit of sugar, soy sauce, and mirin, a sweet rice wine. Heat a square or rectangular tamagoyaki pan over medium heat and lightly oil it.

Pour a thin layer of the egg mixture into the pan, tilting it to spread the eggs evenly. As the eggs begin to set, use chopsticks or a spatula to roll the omelet towards one end of the pan. Add another thin layer of egg to the empty part of the pan, lifting the rolled omelet to let the uncooked egg flow underneath. Continue this process until all the egg mixture is used and you have a neatly rolled omelet. Slice into pieces and serve with a bit of soy sauce or a dash of wasabi for an elegant, flavorful dish.

When it comes to fillings, the possibilities are endless. For a Mediterranean twist, try incorporating ingredients like sun-dried tomatoes, feta cheese, and olives. The briny olives and tangy feta provide a delightful contrast to the creamy eggs. Alternatively, a filling of smoked salmon, cream cheese, and fresh dill can transform your omelet into a sophisticated brunch centerpiece.

For a truly unique take, consider exploring global flavors. An Indian-inspired omelet filled with spiced potatoes, peas, and fresh cilantro offers a burst of vibrant flavors and colors. The spices infuse the eggs with warmth and depth, creating a dish that is both comforting and exciting.

Another inventive approach is to experiment with different types of eggs. Duck eggs, for instance, are larger and richer than chicken eggs, resulting in a more decadent omelet. Quail eggs, while smaller and more delicate, can be used to create individual, bite-sized omelets perfect for appetizers or tapas.

Presentation plays a crucial role in elevating an omelet from simple to sophisticated. Consider using elegant plates and garnishing with fresh herbs, edible flowers, or a sprinkle of finely grated cheese. A light drizzle of high-quality olive oil or a few drops of balsamic reduction can add a touch of finesse. Pairing your omelet with complementary sides, such as a crisp green salad, roasted vegetables, or artisanal bread, can further enhance the dining experience.

Incorporating seasonal ingredients is another way to add sophistication and variety to your omelets. In the spring, fresh asparagus, peas, and mint can provide a burst of freshness. Summer offers an abundance of options, from juicy tomatoes and basil to sweet corn and zucchini. Autumn is the perfect time to incorporate hearty ingredients like squash, kale, and sage, while winter calls for comforting flavors such as roasted root vegetables and rich, creamy cheeses.

Finally, consider the overall dining experience. Whether you're cooking for a special occasion or simply treating yourself to a luxurious breakfast, the ambiance can make a significant difference. Set the table with care, use your favorite dishes, and perhaps light a candle or play some soft music. Taking the time to create a pleasant atmosphere can elevate the enjoyment of your meal.

In conclusion, reinventing the omelet from simple to sophisticated involves mastering basic techniques and embracing creativity. By experimenting with different fillings, presentations, and global flavors, you can transform an everyday dish into a gourmet delight. The versatility of the omelet allows for endless possibilities, making it a canvas for culinary innovation. Whether you prefer a classic French omelet, a hearty Spanish tortilla, or a delicate Japanese tamagoyaki, the key is to approach each variation with an eye for detail and a passion for flavor. With a bit of practice and imagination, you can create omelets that are not only delicious but also a true reflection of your culinary style. Exploring the world of omelets doesn't stop at flavors and techniques. The ingredients you choose can also reflect your culinary vision and the story you want to tell through your cooking. For instance, sourcing local and organic produce can not only enhance the taste and quality of your omelets but also support sustainable practices and local farmers. Imagine an omelet filled with heirloom tomatoes, locally-made goat cheese, and fresh basil picked from your garden. These thoughtful choices contribute to a meal that is both delicious and meaningful.

Modern Takes on Traditional Porridge

Porridge, a dish deeply rooted in many cultures, has evolved significantly over the centuries. Traditionally made from grains such as oats, wheat, or rice simmered in water or milk, porridge has been a staple breakfast food providing warmth and sustenance. Modern culinary practices, however, have breathed new life into this humble dish, transforming it with innovative ingredients, techniques, and presentations while maintaining its comforting essence.

One of the most significant innovations in modern porridge is the use of diverse grains. While oats remain popular, grains such as quinoa, amaranth, farro, and millet have become common additions. These ancient grains not only provide unique textures and flavors but also offer nutritional benefits. Quinoa, for instance, is a complete protein, making it an excellent option for a plant-based diet. Amaranth is rich in calcium and iron, while farro provides a hearty, chewy texture and is high in fiber. By incorporating these grains, modern porridge can be tailored to meet various dietary needs and preferences.

In addition to these grains, seeds and nuts have become popular porridge enhancers. Chia seeds, known for their high omega-3 content, can be soaked and added to porridge for a nutrient boost and a pleasant, gelatinous texture. Flaxseeds, either whole or ground, offer a nutty flavor and are packed with fiber and lignans, which have antioxidant properties. Nuts such as almonds, walnuts, and pecans add crunch and richness, as well as healthy fats and protein. Toasting these nuts before adding them to porridge can enhance their flavor and provide a more complex taste profile.

The liquid used to cook porridge has also seen a transformation. While water and dairy milk are traditional choices, plant-based milks like almond, coconut, and oat milk have become popular alternatives. These options cater to those with lactose intolerance or a preference for vegan diets. Each type of plant-based milk brings its own unique flavor and creaminess to the dish. Coconut milk, for example, adds a tropical twist and a rich, velvety texture, while almond milk provides a subtle nuttiness. Oat milk, with its naturally sweet taste, complements the grains and adds a creamy consistency without overshadowing the other flavors.

Flavorings and sweeteners have also evolved, moving beyond the traditional sugar or honey. Maple syrup, with its deep, caramel-like sweetness, is a favorite modern sweetener. Agave nectar offers a mild, honey-like flavor and has a lower glycemic index, making it a suitable option for those managing blood sugar levels. Date syrup, made from pureed dates, provides natural sweetness along with fiber and minerals like potassium and magnesium. For those seeking a non-sweet option, spices and herbs have become essential. Cinnamon and nutmeg add warmth and depth, while cardamom and ginger bring a hint of exoticism. Fresh herbs like mint or basil can offer a surprising and refreshing twist, especially when paired with fruit or citrus.

Toppings have become an art form in modern porridge making. Fresh fruits, such as berries, bananas, and apples, not only add natural sweetness but also vibrant color and texture. Seasonal fruits can be used to keep the dish exciting throughout the year. In the summer, stone fruits like peaches and plums can be grilled or caramelized for added flavor. In the winter, poached pears or spiced apples can provide warmth and comfort. Dried fruits, such as cranberries, apricots, and raisins, are also popular, offering concentrated sweetness and chewiness. Superfoods like goji berries, cacao nibs, and bee pollen have become trendy additions, each contributing unique flavors and purported health benefits.

Savory porridge has gained popularity as well, providing a hearty and satisfying meal option beyond breakfast. Using broth instead of milk or water, and incorporating ingredients like sautéed vegetables, herbs, and proteins, transforms porridge into a versatile dish suitable for any meal. A savory porridge made with miso broth, topped with mushrooms, spinach, and a poached egg, offers an umami-rich breakfast or lunch option. Another variation could include farro cooked in vegetable broth, mixed with roasted butternut squash, kale, and a drizzle of tahini for a nourishing, plant-based meal.

Modern techniques have also influenced the preparation of porridge. Overnight oats, for example, have become a popular method for those looking for a quick and convenient breakfast option. By soaking oats in milk or a milk alternative overnight, the grains soften and absorb the liquid, creating a creamy, ready-to-eat porridge by morning. This method can be customized with various add-ins such as chia seeds, yogurt, and fresh fruit, allowing for endless variations.

Another innovative technique is the use of slow cookers or instant pots to prepare porridge. These appliances allow for a hands-off cooking experience and can be particularly useful for preparing larger batches. Slow cooking grains overnight in a crockpot results in a rich, creamy porridge that is ready to serve in the morning, while an instant pot can significantly reduce the cooking time for heartier grains like steel-cut oats or farro.

Fermentation has also made its way into modern porridge preparation. By soaking grains in a mixture of water and a bit of whey or yogurt for 12-24 hours before cooking, the grains begin to ferment. This process not only enhances the flavor, giving the porridge a slight tanginess, but also increases the bioavailability of nutrients, making them easier for the body to absorb. Fermented porridge can be a delightful departure from the norm, providing a probiotic boost and a complex flavor profile.

Presentation plays a crucial role in the modern porridge experience. Gone are the days of plain, unadorned bowls. Today, porridge is often served in aesthetically pleasing ways, with careful attention to the arrangement of toppings and the use of colorful ingredients. Layering ingredients, drizzling nut butters or syrups in artistic patterns, and adding edible flowers or herbs can transform a simple bowl of porridge into a visual feast. The use of beautiful bowls and utensils further enhances the dining experience, making the meal feel special and thoughtfully prepared.

Modern takes on traditional porridge also emphasize sustainability and mindfulness. Sourcing organic and locally-grown grains and toppings not only supports local farmers but also ensures the highest quality ingredients. Reducing food waste by using leftover cooked grains from other meals to make porridge is another sustainable practice. Additionally, mindfulness in preparation and consumption—taking the time to savor the process of making porridge and enjoying it slowly—can enhance the overall experience, turning a simple meal into a meditative practice.

Incorporating global influences has also enriched modern porridge recipes. Congee, a traditional Chinese rice porridge, has been embraced and adapted in various ways. Traditionally served with savory toppings like pickled vegetables, meats, and soy sauce, modern versions might include ingredients like avocado, smoked salmon, and sesame seeds. Similarly, Scandinavian-style porridge, known as gröd, often incorporates rye or barley and is served with toppings like skyr (Icelandic yogurt), berries, and nuts. Exploring these global variations can inspire new combinations and flavors, keeping the porridge experience fresh and exciting.

Ultimately, modern takes on traditional porridge celebrate creativity, nutrition, and the joy of cooking. By experimenting with different grains, liquids, flavorings, and toppings, you can transform a simple dish into a personalized culinary masterpiece. Whether you prefer your porridge sweet or savory, hot or cold, there is a world of possibilities waiting to be explored. Embrace the opportunity to reinvent this classic dish and discover new ways to enjoy its comforting and nourishing qualities. Modern porridge also embraces a variety of dietary choices and restrictions, ensuring that everyone can enjoy this versatile dish. For those following a gluten-free diet, grains like rice, quinoa, and buckwheat are excellent alternatives to traditional oats. These grains not only cater to dietary needs but also bring different textures and flavors to the table. A gluten-free porridge made with buckwheat, cooked with almond milk and topped with fresh berries and a drizzle of maple syrup, offers a delightful and nutritious breakfast option.

Fusion Smoothie Bowls

Fusion smoothie bowls have become a vibrant and delicious way to enjoy a blend of flavors and textures from around the world. Combining elements from various culinary traditions, these bowls offer a unique and nutritious meal option that is both visually stunning and satisfying. The concept of fusion in food involves taking ingredients and techniques from different cultures and blending them into a single dish. This approach allows for endless creativity and innovation, making fusion smoothie bowls a perfect canvas for culinary experimentation.

The foundation of any great smoothie bowl is the base. This is typically made from a blend of fruits, vegetables, and liquids, creating a thick and creamy texture that can support a variety of toppings. A common base for fusion smoothie bowls might include a combination of tropical fruits like mango and pineapple with a splash of coconut milk for a touch of the Caribbean. Alternatively, starting with a blend of berries, banana, and almond milk offers a more traditional Western smoothie base, which can be enhanced with spices and flavors from other cuisines.

One popular fusion smoothie bowl base combines the vibrant flavors of Southeast Asia with the creaminess of a classic Western smoothie. By blending frozen mango, banana, and a hint of fresh ginger with coconut milk, you create a tropical yet familiar base. Adding a spoonful of matcha powder, a staple in Japanese cuisine, infuses the bowl with a subtle, earthy flavor and a boost of antioxidants. This blend not only tastes refreshing but also provides a nutritional powerhouse to start your day.

Toppings are where the real magic happens in fusion smoothie bowls. This is your chance to get creative and mix and match ingredients from different culinary traditions. Fresh fruits are a staple topping, adding both sweetness and texture. Consider using slices of kiwi, which bring a tangy flavor and a beautiful green color that contrasts nicely with the yellow-orange base. Blueberries or pomegranate seeds add a burst of color and antioxidants, making the bowl both visually appealing and nutritionally dense.

To add a bit of crunch and complexity, incorporating nuts and seeds from various culinary traditions can be effective. Chopped pistachios, often used in Middle Eastern dishes, provide a rich, buttery flavor and a satisfying crunch. Sesame seeds, whether black or white, are a common ingredient in many Asian cuisines and add a subtle nutty taste. For a bit of Latin

American flair, sprinkle some cacao nibs over the top. These tiny pieces of raw chocolate add a deep, slightly bitter flavor that pairs well with the sweetness of the fruit.

Herbs and spices can elevate the flavor profile of your fusion smoothie bowl. Fresh mint leaves are a versatile addition, offering a burst of freshness that complements both sweet and savory flavors. A sprinkle of cinnamon or cardamom can add warmth and depth, transforming a simple smoothie bowl into an exotic treat. For a touch of South Asian influence, a few saffron threads can be steeped in a bit of warm milk and then drizzled over the top, adding a luxurious aroma and a beautiful golden hue.

Incorporating vegetables into your smoothie bowl not only boosts its nutritional content but also adds interesting flavors and textures. Grated carrots or beets can add natural sweetness and vibrant color, while spinach or kale offers a mild flavor that blends well with fruits. For an even more adventurous twist, try adding a small amount of spirulina, a blue-green algae known for its high protein and nutrient content. While its flavor is quite strong, when used sparingly, spirulina can turn your smoothie bowl a striking shade of blue or green.

Another exciting approach to fusion smoothie bowls is to draw inspiration from traditional desserts from around the world. For instance, a smoothie bowl inspired by the classic Indian dessert, kulfi, can be created by blending frozen banana, mango, and a splash of rose water. Topping it with chopped pistachios, a sprinkle of cardamom, and a drizzle of honey transforms the bowl into a decadent treat that echoes the flavors of this beloved dessert.

If you're a fan of the flavors of Latin America, consider a smoothie bowl inspired by the traditional Mexican beverage, horchata. Start with a base of almond milk and blend in frozen banana, a touch of vanilla extract, and a generous sprinkle of cinnamon. Top this creamy, spiced base with slices of fresh banana, a handful of granola, and a sprinkle of cinnamon sugar for a bowl that captures the essence of horchata in a refreshing, nutritious form.

Fusion smoothie bowls can also take inspiration from savory dishes, creating a unique and unexpected flavor experience. A Mediterranean-inspired bowl might start with a base of blended cucumber, spinach, and a touch of Greek yogurt, creating a refreshing and light green smoothie. Topping this with cherry tomatoes, crumbled feta cheese, olives, and a drizzle of olive oil results in a savory smoothie bowl that is both filling and packed with flavor.

Exploring the flavors of East Asia can lead to some truly unique fusion smoothie bowls. A base of blended pineapple, banana, and a splash of coconut milk can be transformed with the addition of a small amount of miso paste. This savory ingredient, commonly used in Japanese cuisine, adds a depth of flavor that is unexpected but delicious. Topped with sliced avocado, sesame seeds, and a sprinkling of nori flakes, this smoothie bowl offers a delightful mix of sweet, savory, and umami flavors.

Another fusion approach involves incorporating superfoods and health-boosting ingredients from various cultures. Acai berries from Brazil, known for their high antioxidant content, can be blended into the base of your smoothie bowl. Adding a spoonful of turmeric, a staple in Indian cuisine, provides anti-inflammatory benefits and a beautiful golden color. Spirulina from the sea, chia seeds from Mexico, and goji berries from China can all be incorporated as toppings, creating a global superfood smoothie bowl that is as nutritious as it is delicious.

To make your fusion smoothie bowl truly your own, consider the textural elements you enjoy most. If you love a bit of crunch, granola, toasted coconut flakes, or even crispy rice can be excellent additions. For a smoother texture, a dollop of nut butter or a swirl of yogurt can add creaminess and richness. The key to a successful fusion smoothie bowl is balance—balancing flavors, textures, and colors to create a harmonious and satisfying meal.

Preparation techniques can also play a role in creating the perfect fusion smoothie bowl. Freezing fruits and vegetables before blending ensures a thick and creamy consistency, almost like a soft-serve ice cream. Using a high-speed blender can help achieve a smooth texture, while layering ingredients can create a visually appealing presentation. Taking the time to arrange toppings thoughtfully not only makes the bowl more attractive but also enhances the eating experience, allowing you to savor each bite.

Fusion smoothie bowls are a testament to the endless possibilities of culinary creativity. By blending ingredients and techniques from different cultures, you can create a dish that is both familiar and new, comforting and exciting. Whether you draw inspiration from traditional desserts, savory dishes, or superfoods from around the world, the fusion smoothie bowl offers a delicious and nutritious way to explore the flavors of the globe. Embrace the opportunity to experiment and discover your own favorite combinations, turning each smoothie bowl into a culinary adventure. One of the great joys of creating fusion smoothie bowls is the ability to tailor them to your personal tastes and dietary needs. If you are following a plant-based diet, there are countless options to explore. Using plant-based milks like almond, soy, or oat milk as the base can provide a creamy texture without dairy. Adding protein-rich ingredients such as hemp seeds, chia seeds, or a scoop of plant-based protein powder can ensure your smoothie bowl is as filling as it is flavorful.

Breakfast Pastries: Old Meets New

Breakfast pastries have long held a cherished place in culinary traditions around the world. From the flaky croissants of France to the dense, sweet cinnamon rolls of Scandinavia, these morning delights offer comfort, indulgence, and a sense of tradition. Yet, as our tastes and dietary preferences evolve, so too do the pastries we enjoy. The fusion of old-world techniques with modern twists has given rise to a new generation of breakfast pastries that honor their origins while embracing contemporary flavors and ingredients.

The croissant, with its buttery layers and delicate crispness, remains a cornerstone of breakfast pastries. Its origins date back to Austria, where it was first created as the kipferl, a crescent-shaped bread. The French later adopted and perfected the technique, giving us the croissant we know today. Modern bakers have taken this classic and infused it with new flavors and fillings, creating variations like the almond croissant, filled with sweet almond paste and topped with sliced almonds, or the pain au chocolat, which encases rich, dark chocolate within its folds.

In recent years, croissant hybrids have emerged, blending the traditional pastry with unexpected elements. The cronut, a cross between a croissant and a donut, exemplifies this trend. Created by Dominique Ansel in New York City, the cronut features the laminated dough of a croissant, deep-fried like a donut, and often filled with various creams or jams. This innovative pastry has sparked a wave of similar creations, each offering a unique twist on the beloved croissant.

Danish pastries, or danishes, are another staple of breakfast pastry menus. These pastries, with their laminated dough and sweet fillings, originated in Denmark but have become popular worldwide. Traditional danishes often feature fillings like fruit preserves, cream cheese, or almond paste. Modern interpretations have expanded the range of fillings to include ingredients like matcha green tea, dulce de leche, or savory options such as spinach and feta. This blend of old and new keeps the danish relevant and exciting, appealing to both traditionalists and adventurous eaters.

Cinnamon rolls, with their spiraled layers of dough, cinnamon sugar, and icing, offer a comforting sweetness that is hard to resist. Originating in Sweden, where they are known as kanelbullar, these pastries have been embraced and adapted by cultures around the world. In the United States, the classic cinnamon roll is often topped with a thick layer of cream cheese frosting, adding a tangy contrast to the sweet filling. Contemporary variations might incorporate additional ingredients like pecans, raisins, or even bacon for a savory-sweet twist.

Scones, a staple of British tea time, have also found a place at the breakfast table. Traditionally made with flour, butter, sugar, and milk or cream, scones can be either sweet or savory. Classic sweet scones often include currants or raisins and are served with clotted cream and jam. Modern versions might feature ingredients like chocolate chips, blueberries, or even lavender. Savory scones, on the other hand, might include cheddar cheese, chives, or sun-dried tomatoes, offering a hearty alternative to their sweet counterparts.

The fusion of old and new is evident in the resurgence of interest in artisanal baking techniques. Sourdough, a method that dates back thousands of years, has seen a revival in recent years. Bakers are now incorporating sourdough into their pastry recipes, adding a depth of flavor and a natural leavening process that enhances the texture and taste of the final product. Sourdough croissants, for example, offer a tangy twist on the classic, while sourdough cinnamon rolls have a slightly chewy texture that sets them apart from their yeasted counterparts.

Another trend in modern breakfast pastries is the incorporation of global flavors and ingredients. Matcha, a finely ground green tea powder from Japan, has become a popular addition to pastries, lending its vibrant color and earthy flavor to everything from croissants to muffins. Tahini, a sesame seed paste commonly used in Middle Eastern cuisine, adds a rich, nutty flavor to cookies and cakes. Incorporating these ingredients into traditional pastry recipes creates a fusion that is both familiar and novel, appealing to a wide range of palates.

Health-conscious consumers have also influenced the evolution of breakfast pastries. Bakers are increasingly experimenting with alternative flours, such as almond, coconut, or spelt, to create gluten-free options. Natural sweeteners like honey, maple syrup, or coconut sugar are being used in place of refined sugars, offering a more wholesome way to enjoy sweet treats. These adaptations allow those with dietary restrictions or preferences to enjoy the pleasure of a freshly baked pastry without compromising on flavor or quality.

The visual appeal of breakfast pastries has also evolved, with bakers paying close attention to presentation and aesthetics. The art of pastry decoration has reached new heights, with intricate designs, vibrant colors, and creative garnishes. A simple croissant might be topped with edible flowers, a danish draped with a delicate glaze, or a scone dusted with a shimmering layer of powdered sugar. These visual enhancements not only make the pastries more enticing but also reflect the care and craftsmanship that go into their creation.

One cannot overlook the impact of cultural exchanges on the world of breakfast pastries. The global nature of modern cuisine means that flavors and techniques from one part of the world can easily influence another. For example, the incorporation of spices like cardamom and saffron, traditionally used in Middle Eastern and South Asian desserts, can add a fragrant complexity to pastries. The use of tropical fruits like mango, passion fruit, or guava can infuse a burst of exotic flavor into muffins or danishes, creating a delightful cross-cultural experience.

The rise of small-batch and artisanal bakeries has also played a significant role in the renaissance of breakfast pastries. These bakeries often prioritize quality ingredients, traditional techniques, and innovative flavor combinations, setting themselves apart from mass-produced options. The personal touch and attention to detail found in these establishments ensure that each pastry is a work of art, reflecting the baker's passion and creativity.

In embracing the fusion of old and new, breakfast pastries continue to captivate our senses and bring joy to our mornings. The delicate balance of tradition and innovation allows these beloved treats to evolve while honoring their roots. Whether you prefer the classic simplicity of a buttery croissant or the adventurous flavors of a matcha-infused danish, the world of breakfast pastries offers something for everyone. As we continue to explore and experiment, one thing remains certain: the timeless appeal of a freshly baked pastry, enjoyed with a cup of coffee or tea, is a pleasure that will never go out of style. The timeless appeal of breakfast pastries also lies in their ability to bring people together. The act of sharing a warm, freshly baked pastry with loved ones creates moments of connection and joy. Whether it's a leisurely weekend brunch, a quick weekday breakfast, or a special occasion, pastries have a way of making any moment feel a bit more special. This communal aspect is a significant part of why these treats have been cherished across generations and cultures.

Chapter 3

Appetizers and Starters

Timeless Soups with a Contemporary Flair

Soup, a culinary staple that spans centuries and cultures, has always been a comforting, nourishing, and versatile dish. From hearty stews that sustained ancient civilizations to elegant consommés served in fine dining, the evolution of soup reflects both our history and our innovation. Today, the challenge and excitement lie in blending these timeless recipes with contemporary flavors and techniques, creating bowls that honor tradition while embracing modern palates.

Consider the humble chicken soup, a classic that has been a remedy for colds and a comfort food for generations. Traditionally made with a simple broth, vegetables, and tender chicken pieces, it is a dish steeped in nostalgia. However, modern interpretations elevate this staple by incorporating global influences and novel ingredients. Imagine a chicken soup infused with lemongrass, ginger, and coconut milk, transforming it into a vibrant Thai-inspired dish. This fusion not only adds depth and complexity but also introduces a refreshing twist while maintaining the soul-soothing essence of the original.

Another example of this blend of old and new is the traditional French onion soup. Known for its rich beef broth, caramelized onions, and a topping of crusty bread and melted Gruyère cheese, this soup is a testament to the French culinary technique. Contemporary chefs might enhance this classic by adding a splash of sherry or red wine for added depth, experimenting with different cheeses for the gratinée, or even using a vegetarian broth to cater to diverse dietary preferences. These adjustments respect the integrity of the dish while making it accessible and exciting to a broader audience.

Tomato soup, another timeless favorite, often conjures images of a simple, creamy bowl paired with a grilled cheese sandwich. The classic version is straightforward, relying on the natural sweetness of ripe tomatoes, a touch of cream, and the fragrant notes of basil. Modern renditions might roast the tomatoes to concentrate their flavor, add a hint of smoked paprika for a subtle kick, or substitute dairy with coconut milk to create a vegan-friendly option. Each variation offers a new experience while preserving the comforting familiarity of the original.

Moving beyond Western traditions, consider the Japanese miso soup, a staple in Japanese cuisine known for its umami-rich broth made from fermented soybean paste. Traditionally, it includes tofu, seaweed, and green onions. Modern adaptations might incorporate a variety of mushrooms for added texture and flavor, or use miso as a base for a heartier stew with vegetables and noodles. This approach not only broadens the appeal of miso soup but also showcases the versatility of miso as an ingredient.

Italian minestrone soup, a hearty vegetable soup with beans and pasta, is another classic that lends itself well to contemporary twists. The traditional version is a celebration of seasonal vegetables, simmered in a tomato-based broth with herbs like basil and oregano. Modern chefs might play with this by incorporating grains like quinoa or farro instead of pasta, using kale or Swiss chard for a nutritional boost, or adding a dollop of pesto for an unexpected burst of flavor. These variations keep the essence of minestrone intact while offering new textures and tastes.

The concept of blending old and new extends to techniques as well. Traditional soups often relied on slow simmering to develop flavors, a method that remains effective but can be time-consuming. Modern technology, such as pressure cookers and instant pots, allows for the same depth of flavor in a fraction of the time. For example, a classic beef stew that might take hours to cook on the stove can be ready in under an hour with a pressure cooker, without sacrificing the rich, hearty flavors that are characteristic of this dish.

Incorporating contemporary dietary trends is another way to modernize timeless soups. The rise of plant-based diets has led to creative vegetable-forward soups that are both nutritious and delicious. A traditional potato leek soup, for instance, can be made vegan by using vegetable broth and coconut milk instead of chicken broth and cream. Adding nutritional yeast can provide a cheesy flavor without dairy, making the soup accessible to those with dietary restrictions while still delivering a satisfying, comforting bowl.

The visual presentation of soups has also evolved, with chefs paying more attention to aesthetics. Traditional soups were often rustic and unadorned, served as they were cooked. Today, a garnish of fresh herbs, a drizzle of flavored oil, or a sprinkle of seeds can elevate the visual appeal of a soup, making it not only a delight to eat but also a feast for the eyes. This attention to detail reflects the contemporary focus on not just flavor but the overall dining experience.

The sustainability movement has also influenced modern soup-making practices. Using locally sourced, seasonal ingredients not only supports local farmers but also ensures the freshest and most flavorful produce. Reducing food waste by utilizing vegetable scraps and bones for broth is another practice that aligns with sustainable cooking. These modern considerations add an ethical dimension to the timeless practice of soup-making, marrying tradition with responsibility.

Storytelling through food is another compelling aspect of contemporary soup-making. Each bowl can tell a story of cultural heritage, personal history, or innovative experimentation. A soup might be inspired by a childhood memory, a travel experience, or a desire to recreate a beloved dish with a new twist. Sharing these stories can deepen the connection between the cook and the diner, turning a simple meal into a meaningful experience.

The enduring popularity of soups lies in their ability to adapt and evolve while providing comfort and nourishment. By blending timeless recipes with contemporary flair, we can create soups that honor their origins yet feel fresh and exciting. This approach not only keeps traditional dishes relevant but also invites new generations to appreciate and enjoy them. Whether through the infusion of global flavors, the incorporation of modern techniques, or the attention to dietary trends and sustainability, the world of soups offers endless possibilities for creativity and connection.

In the end, the essence of soup remains unchanged: it is a dish that brings warmth, comfort, and sustenance. The marriage of old and new in soup-making enriches our culinary landscape, offering a delicious way to celebrate tradition while exploring innovation. So, the next time you ladle a steaming bowl of soup, take a moment to savor not just the flavors but the history, creativity, and care that have come together to create that perfect, timeless dish. The beauty of soups lies in their ability to transcend seasons and occasions. For instance, in the chill of winter, nothing is more comforting than a bowl of hearty vegetable soup, rich with root vegetables, legumes, and aromatic herbs. The traditional winter vegetable soup can be infused with contemporary flair by adding unexpected ingredients like roasted garlic, smoked paprika, or even a touch of harissa for warmth and complexity.

Updated Hors oeuvres: Small Bites, Big Flavor

Hors d'oeuvres, those delightful little bites that often precede a meal, have evolved significantly over the years. Once simple canapés or cheese and crackers, these small bites have become canvases for chefs and home cooks alike to showcase creativity, skill, and global influences. Today, hors d'oeuvres are not just appetizers; they are an integral part of culinary experiences, capable of setting the tone for an entire meal with their bold flavors and artistic presentation.

Imagine walking into a party and being greeted by a tray of beautifully arranged hors d'oeuvres, each one a miniature masterpiece. The first bite you take is a smoked salmon mousse on a cucumber round, garnished with a sprig of dill and a caper berry. The freshness of the cucumber, the richness of the salmon, and the briny pop of the caper create a symphony of flavors that dance on your palate. This modern take on a classic combination exemplifies how contemporary hors d'oeuvres can elevate traditional ingredients.

Another prime example is the ubiquitous bruschetta. Traditionally, it is a simple preparation of toasted bread rubbed with garlic and topped with fresh tomatoes, basil, and olive oil. In its updated form, bruschetta can transform into a sophisticated bite by using heirloom cherry tomatoes, balsamic reduction, and a touch of burrata cheese. The sweet acidity of the tomatoes, the creamy richness of the burrata, and the tangy balsamic glaze come together in perfect harmony, offering a fresh take on a beloved classic.

The influence of global cuisines has profoundly impacted the world of hors d'oeuvres, introducing a plethora of flavors and techniques. Consider the Vietnamese spring roll, a light and refreshing appetizer traditionally filled with shrimp, rice noodles, and fresh herbs, and served with a peanut dipping sauce. Modern versions might incorporate unexpected fillings such as spicy tuna tartare with avocado, or grilled lemongrass chicken with mango salsa. These variations maintain the essence of the original dish while introducing contemporary flair and cross-cultural influences.

Another great example is the Spanish tapas tradition, which offers a wealth of inspiration for modern hors d'oeuvres. Classic tapas like patatas bravas or croquettes can be reimagined with gourmet twists. For instance, patatas bravas, typically fried potatoes with a spicy tomato sauce, can be served as crispy potato nests with a smoky paprika aioli and microgreens. Croquettes, often filled with ham or chicken, can be elevated by using ingredients like truffle oil, wild mushrooms, or gourmet cheeses. These updates not only enhance the flavor profile but also add a touch of elegance to these traditional bites.

Sushi, with its precise and artful presentation, has also influenced the modern hors d'oeuvre scene. Sushi-inspired hors d'oeuvres can range from deconstructed sushi bowls served in mini ramekins to sushi rolls reimagined with unconventional fillings like quinoa, roasted vegetables, or even foie gras. These adaptations respect the meticulous nature of sushi-making while exploring new textures and flavors that appeal to contemporary tastes.

The trend of farm-to-table has also left its mark on hors d'oeuvres, emphasizing the use of fresh, locally sourced ingredients. Imagine a bite-sized caprese salad made with cherry tomatoes, fresh basil, and locally produced mozzarella, drizzled with extra virgin olive oil and a pinch of sea salt. This simple yet elegant hors d'oeuvre highlights the quality of the ingredients and the beauty of seasonal produce.

Similarly, a small skewer of grilled seasonal vegetables, marinated in herbs and olive oil, can capture the essence of a summer garden in a single bite.

Molecular gastronomy has further expanded the boundaries of what hors d'oeuvres can be. Techniques like spherification, foaming, and sous-vide cooking have introduced new textures and presentations that intrigue and delight diners. Imagine a tomato and basil "caviar" served on a Parmesan crisp, where the tomato essence bursts in your mouth, leaving a lingering taste of fresh herbs. These innovative approaches transform familiar flavors into extraordinary experiences, pushing the envelope of culinary creativity.

The rise of dietary awareness and preferences has also shaped modern hors d'oeuvres. Gluten-free, vegan, and keto-friendly options are now readily available, ensuring that all guests can enjoy these small bites regardless of dietary restrictions. For instance, a vegan hors d'oeuvre might feature cashew cheese and roasted red pepper on a slice of cucumber, offering a rich and satisfying alternative to traditional cheese-based canapés. A gluten-free option could be a mini polenta cake topped with wild mushrooms and a drizzle of truffle oil, providing a luxurious bite without the gluten.

Presentation plays a crucial role in the appeal of hors d'oeuvres. The visual impact of these small bites can enhance the overall dining experience, making them not just tasty but also Instagram-worthy. Using vibrant colors, contrasting textures, and elegant plating techniques can make even the simplest ingredients look and feel special. A beautifully arranged charcuterie board, for example, can be elevated with artistic garnishes and thoughtful pairings of meats, cheeses, fruits, and nuts.

The social aspect of hors d'oeuvres cannot be overlooked. These small bites are perfect for mingling, allowing guests to sample a variety of flavors while engaging in conversation. They encourage a relaxed and convivial atmosphere, where the formality of a sit-down meal is replaced by the joy of shared experiences and culinary exploration. The versatility of hors d'oeuvres makes them ideal for any occasion, from casual gatherings to elegant soirées.

Practicality and preparation are key when it comes to creating hors d'oeuvres. Many can be prepared ahead of time, allowing hosts to enjoy their own parties without being tied to the kitchen. Cold hors d'oeuvres like ceviche or tartare can be made a few hours in advance and served straight from the fridge. Warm options like mini quiches or stuffed mushrooms can be prepped and then baked just before serving. This flexibility ensures that hors d'oeuvres are not only delicious but also convenient for entertaining.

In conclusion, the world of hors d'oeuvres has evolved into a realm of endless possibilities, where tradition meets innovation and global flavors converge. These small bites, with their big flavors, set the stage for memorable meals and gatherings. By embracing contemporary techniques, sourcing high-quality ingredients, and paying attention to presentation, anyone can create hors d'oeuvres that are not only delectable but also visually stunning. Whether you're hosting an intimate dinner or a grand celebration, these updated hors d'oeuvres will leave a lasting impression on your guests, showcasing your culinary prowess and creativity in every bite. One of the most exciting aspects of modern hors d'oeuvres is the ability to play with unexpected flavor combinations and textures. Take, for instance, the classic pairing of sweet and savory elements. A bite-sized piece of prosciutto-wrapped melon is a timeless favorite, but adding a drizzle of balsamic reduction or a sprinkle of fresh mint can elevate this simple dish into something truly special. The sweetness of the melon, the saltiness of the prosciutto, and the acidity of the balsamic create a balanced and intriguing flavor profile that delights the palate.

Salads: Traditional Bases, Modern Dressings

Salads, with their vibrant colors and fresh ingredients, have long been a staple in diets around the world. Traditionally, salads are built on a foundation of greens and vegetables, but modern interpretations have expanded these bases to include grains, legumes, and even fruits. The real transformation, however, comes with the dressings. Contemporary dressings have evolved beyond simple vinaigrettes, incorporating bold flavors and unique ingredients that elevate the humble salad to an extraordinary culinary experience.

Think back to the classic Caesar salad, a perennial favorite that combines crunchy romaine lettuce, creamy dressing, Parmesan cheese, and croutons. While delicious in its traditional form, the Caesar salad can be reimagined with a modern twist. Consider swapping the romaine for kale, a nutrient-dense green that offers a robust texture. The dressing can be updated by blending Greek yogurt with anchovies, garlic, lemon juice, and a dash of Worcestershire sauce, creating a lighter yet equally flavorful alternative. Adding roasted chickpeas instead of croutons introduces a crunchy element and boosts the protein content, making for a more balanced dish.

Another traditional base is the Caprese salad, which features ripe tomatoes, fresh mozzarella, and basil, typically drizzled with olive oil and balsamic vinegar. To modernize this classic, try using heirloom tomatoes of various colors and sizes for a visually striking presentation. Burrata cheese, with its creamy interior, can substitute for mozzarella, adding an extra layer of indulgence. Instead of the standard balsamic vinegar, a balsamic reduction or even a splash of aged balsamic can provide a richer, more concentrated flavor. Garnishing with microgreens or edible flowers not only enhances the dish's visual appeal but also introduces subtle new flavors.

Grain-based salads have gained popularity for their heartiness and nutritional benefits. A traditional tabbouleh, for instance, is made with bulgur, parsley, mint, tomatoes, and cucumbers, dressed with lemon juice and olive oil. To give this Middle Eastern staple a modern twist, you can replace the bulgur with quinoa, which is high in protein and has a pleasant, nutty flavor. Additions like pomegranate seeds or dried apricots can introduce a sweet contrast, while a handful of toasted nuts or seeds adds crunch and depth. The dressing can be spiced up with a touch of sumac or za'atar, lending an exotic flair to the familiar dish.

Legume-based salads also offer a versatile foundation. The traditional three-bean salad, typically made with kidney beans, green beans, and chickpeas, can be revitalized with contemporary ingredients. Consider using a mix of different beans such as black beans, cannellini beans, and edamame for varied textures and colors. A dressing made with lime juice, cilantro, cumin, and a hint of chili powder can infuse the salad with a vibrant, Southwestern-inspired flavor. Adding diced avocado and cherry tomatoes not only enhances the nutritional profile but also adds creaminess and freshness.

Fruit is another excellent base for modern salads, offering a sweet and refreshing contrast to savory elements. A traditional Waldorf salad combines apples, celery, grapes, and walnuts in a mayonnaise-based dressing. Updating this classic can involve using Greek yogurt instead of mayonnaise for a healthier twist. Adding ingredients like arugula or spinach can provide a peppery counterpoint to the sweet fruit. A dressing made with honey, lemon juice, and a hint of Dijon mustard can bring all the flavors together in a harmonious blend.

Modern dressings have become the cornerstone of contemporary salads, transforming simple ingredients into sophisticated dishes. One popular trend is the use of emulsified dressings that combine oil and vinegar or citrus juice with other flavorful components. For instance, a honey-mustard dressing can be made by whisking together Dijon mustard, honey, apple cider vinegar, and olive oil. This sweet and tangy dressing pairs beautifully with bitter greens like arugula or radicchio, balancing their sharp flavors.

Another innovative dressing is the avocado-lime dressing, perfect for Southwest-inspired salads. Blending ripe avocado with lime juice, cilantro, garlic, and a touch of olive oil creates a creamy, rich dressing that is both dairy-free and packed with healthy fats. This dressing works wonderfully with salads featuring black beans, corn, and grilled chicken, adding a luscious texture and zesty flavor.

Tahini-based dressings have also gained popularity, especially in Middle Eastern and Mediterranean salads. A simple tahini dressing can be made by mixing tahini with lemon juice, garlic, water, and a pinch of salt. This creamy, nutty dressing complements salads with roasted vegetables, chickpeas, and fresh herbs. For a spicier version, adding a touch of harissa or smoked paprika can introduce a warm, smoky element that enhances the overall flavor profile.

Asian-inspired dressings offer another avenue for creative salad compositions. A miso-ginger dressing, for example, can be made by blending white miso paste with rice vinegar, fresh ginger, soy sauce, and sesame oil. This umami-rich dressing pairs well with crunchy vegetables like cabbage, carrots, and bell peppers, as well as proteins like tofu or grilled shrimp. The complex flavors of the dressing elevate the salad, making it a standout dish.

For those who enjoy a bit of sweetness in their salads, fruit-based dressings provide a delightful option. A raspberry vinaigrette, made by pureeing fresh or frozen raspberries with balsamic vinegar, honey, and olive oil, offers a vibrant, fruity flavor that complements salads with mixed greens, goat cheese, and candied pecans. Similarly, a mango-cilantro dressing can be created by blending ripe mango with lime juice, cilantro, and a splash of olive oil. This tropical dressing is perfect for salads featuring grilled shrimp or chicken, avocado, and red onion.

The versatility of modern dressings means that they can be tailored to suit any dietary preference or restriction. For vegan dressings, ingredients like nutritional yeast, cashews, and coconut milk can be used to create creamy, flavorful alternatives to dairy-based dressings. A cashew cream dressing, for instance, can be made by soaking cashews and then blending them with lemon juice, garlic, and water until smooth. This rich, dairy-free dressing pairs well with hearty salads featuring roasted vegetables and grains.

Incorporating herbs and spices into dressings is another way to enhance flavor and add a unique twist. Fresh herbs like basil, mint, and dill can be blended into dressings to infuse them with bright, aromatic notes. Spices like cumin, coriander, and smoked paprika can add depth and warmth, transforming a simple vinaigrette into a complex, flavorful dressing.

Ultimately, the key to creating memorable salads lies in the balance of flavors, textures, and colors. By starting with a traditional base and experimenting with modern dressings, you can elevate your salad game and delight your taste buds. Whether you're crafting a light, refreshing salad for a summer lunch or a hearty, nourishing salad for dinner, the possibilities are endless. Embrace the creativity and versatility of salads, and let your imagination guide you in creating dishes that are not only nutritious but also bursting with flavor and visual appeal. Experimentation can extend beyond just the ingredients and dressings to the methods of preparation. Roasting or grilling vegetables before adding them to your salad can impart a depth of flavor that raw vegetables simply can't achieve. For instance, roasted beets, sweet potatoes, and carrots bring out natural sweetness and a caramelized texture that can transform a simple mixed greens salad into a gourmet dish. Pair these roasted vegetables with a tangy goat cheese, a handful of toasted nuts, and a robust vinaigrette to create a salad that's both hearty and satisfying.

Classic Dips and Spreads with a Twist

Dips and spreads have long been a beloved staple in the culinary world, offering versatile and flavorful options for appetizers, snacks, and even meal enhancements. Classics like hummus, guacamole, and tzatziki have graced many a table, but giving these familiar favorites a modern twist can elevate them to new culinary heights. This chapter explores innovative ways to refresh these classic dips and spreads, infusing them with contemporary flavors and ingredients that surprise and delight.

Hummus, a traditional Middle Eastern dip made from chickpeas, tahini, lemon juice, and garlic, is a great canvas for creativity. To put a modern spin on this classic, consider incorporating roasted vegetables like red peppers, beets, or sweet potatoes. Roasting these vegetables brings out their natural sweetness and adds a depth of flavor to the hummus. For instance, roasted red pepper hummus not only boasts a vibrant color but also a smoky, sweet undertone that complements the earthiness of the chickpeas. To make it, blend roasted red peppers with the traditional hummus ingredients, adjusting the seasoning to taste.

Another twist on hummus involves using different legumes. Black bean hummus, for example, offers a hearty, slightly smoky flavor that pairs well with lime juice and cumin. The process is similar to making traditional hummus but substituting black beans for chickpeas. Adding ingredients like cilantro and jalapeño can give it a Southwestern flair, making it a perfect accompaniment for tortilla chips or vegetable sticks.

Guacamole, the beloved avocado-based dip, is another classic that lends itself well to innovation. While the traditional version includes avocado, lime juice, cilantro, onion, and jalapeño, adding unexpected ingredients can create exciting new flavors. One such variation is mango guacamole. The sweetness of ripe mangoes contrasts beautifully with the creamy avocado and the heat from the jalapeño, creating a well-balanced dip that's both refreshing and satisfying. Simply fold diced mango into your guacamole and adjust the other ingredients to taste.

For a more robust guacamole, consider adding roasted corn and black beans. This version adds texture and heartiness, making it almost a meal in itself. The roasted corn adds a sweet, smoky flavor, while the black beans contribute protein and a satisfying bite. This variation is perfect for topping tacos, spreading on toast, or simply serving with your favorite chips.

Tzatziki, a traditional Greek dip made from yogurt, cucumber, garlic, and dill, is a refreshing and tangy accompaniment to many dishes. To give tzatziki a modern twist, try incorporating different herbs and spices. Mint and basil can add a fresh, aromatic quality, while a touch of smoked paprika or cumin can introduce a subtle warmth and complexity. For a richer version, consider using a mix of Greek yogurt and sour cream, which adds a luxurious creaminess to the dip.

Another innovative approach to tzatziki is to use different base ingredients. Avocado tzatziki, for example, combines the creaminess of avocados with the tang of yogurt, creating a dip that's both rich and refreshing. Blend avocados with Greek yogurt, lemon juice, garlic, and herbs for a unique take on this classic dip. This version pairs wonderfully with grilled meats, vegetables, or as a spread on sandwiches.

Spinach and artichoke dip is a classic American favorite, often served warm and gooey with plenty of cheese. To modernize this beloved dip, consider incorporating more vegetables and using lighter ingredients. For a healthier version, substitute some of the cheese and mayonnaise with Greek yogurt and puréed cauliflower. This not only reduces the calorie content but also adds a subtle, earthy flavor that complements the spinach and artichokes. Adding roasted garlic or sun-dried tomatoes can introduce new layers of flavor, making the dip more complex and interesting.

Baba ganoush, a smoky, creamy eggplant dip from the Middle East, is another classic that can benefit from a modern twist. Traditional baba ganoush includes roasted eggplant, tahini, lemon juice, and garlic. To add a contemporary flair, try incorporating additional roasted vegetables like bell peppers or tomatoes. These additions can enhance the dip's sweetness and complexity. For a spicier version, adding a touch of harissa or smoked paprika can introduce a warm, smoky heat that complements the eggplant's natural flavor.

Cheese spreads are another area ripe for innovation. A classic pimento cheese spread, traditionally made with cheddar cheese, pimentos, mayonnaise, and seasonings, can be modernized with the addition of unexpected ingredients. Roasted jalapeños can add a spicy kick, while smoked gouda can introduce a rich, smoky flavor. For a more sophisticated version, consider incorporating fresh herbs like chives and parsley, which add a bright, fresh element to the spread.

Pesto, while traditionally made with basil, pine nuts, Parmesan cheese, and olive oil, can be easily adapted to include a variety of herbs and nuts. Arugula and walnut pesto, for example, offers a peppery, nutty alternative to the classic. The process remains the same: blend the arugula, walnuts, Parmesan, garlic, and olive oil until smooth. This variation pairs well with pasta, grilled meats, or as a spread on sandwiches.

Another exciting twist on pesto is sun-dried tomato pesto. This version combines sun-dried tomatoes, basil, almonds, Parmesan, and olive oil, creating a rich, tangy spread that's bursting with flavor. The sun-dried tomatoes add a concentrated sweetness that pairs beautifully with the savory almonds and cheese. This pesto works wonderfully as a pasta sauce, a spread for bruschetta, or a dip for vegetables.

Experimenting with different cultural influences can also lead to exciting new dips and spreads. For example, a Mexican-inspired corn dip can combine grilled corn, cotija cheese, lime juice, and cilantro, creating a tangy, creamy dip with a hint of smokiness. This dip is perfect for serving with tortilla chips or as a topping for tacos and grilled meats.

An Asian-inspired edamame dip offers another unique option. Blending cooked edamame with garlic, ginger, soy sauce, and sesame oil creates a smooth, flavorful dip that's both healthy and delicious. Adding a touch of wasabi or sriracha can introduce a spicy kick, making this dip perfect for serving with rice crackers or vegetable sticks.

Incorporating seasonal ingredients can also inspire innovative dips and spreads. A roasted pumpkin and sage dip, for example, combines the earthy sweetness of roasted pumpkin with the aromatic quality of fresh sage. Blended with a touch of cream cheese and Parmesan, this dip becomes a rich, savory spread that's perfect for autumn gatherings. Serve it with crusty bread or crackers for a comforting, seasonal appetizer.

Another seasonal option is a strawberry and basil cream cheese spread. Fresh strawberries and basil are blended with cream cheese and a touch of honey, creating a sweet, tangy spread that's perfect for summer. This spread can be served with bagels, crackers, or as a topping for desserts like cheesecake or pound cake.

The possibilities for modernizing classic dips and spreads are endless. By experimenting with different ingredients, flavors, and textures, you can create unique and exciting versions of old favorites. Whether you're hosting a party, preparing a snack, or looking to add a flavorful touch to your meals, these innovative dips and spreads are sure to impress and delight. The key is to balance familiar elements with new, unexpected twists, creating dishes that are both comforting and adventurous. A classic spread that often makes an appearance at gatherings is pâté. Traditionally made with liver, butter, and seasonings, this rich and creamy spread offers numerous opportunities for a modern twist. For a lighter version, consider making a mushroom pâté. Sauté a variety of mushrooms with garlic and shallots until they're deeply caramelized, then blend them with cream cheese or Greek yogurt for creaminess. Adding a splash of sherry or white wine can enhance the flavors, and fresh herbs like thyme or parsley can brighten the dish. This vegetarian alternative provides the same luxurious texture as traditional pâté but with a fresh, earthy flavor.

Revamped Canapés for Modern Palates

Canapés, those small, decorative finger foods served at parties and receptions, have undergone a significant transformation in recent years. Once dominated by predictable combinations, today's canapés cater to a diverse range of tastes and dietary preferences. This chapter delves into the art of creating revamped canapés that appeal to modern palates, emphasizing innovative ingredients, presentation techniques, and flavor profiles.

A crucial aspect of modern canapés is the emphasis on fresh, high-quality ingredients. Gone are the days when processed meats and cheeses reigned supreme. Instead, today's canapés often feature seasonal produce, artisanal cheeses, and sustainably sourced proteins. This shift not only enhances the flavor and nutritional value but also aligns with the growing consumer demand for transparency and sustainability in food production.

One popular approach in modern canapé creation is the use of plant-based ingredients. With the rise of vegetarian and vegan diets, incorporating plant-based options has become essential. Think of vibrant, roasted vegetable tarts, where a flaky pastry base is topped with a medley of caramelized onions, bell peppers, and zucchini, finished with a drizzle of balsamic glaze. These canapés are not only visually appealing but also packed with flavor and nutrients. Another example is the use of legumes and grains, such as quinoa-stuffed mini bell peppers or chickpea and avocado bites on cucumber rounds. These options provide a satisfying and protein-rich alternative to traditional meat-based canapés.

Innovative presentations also play a significant role in modernizing canapés. The visual appeal of a dish can be as important as its taste, especially in the age of social media where food photography is ubiquitous. Using colorful ingredients, unique serving vessels, and creative garnishes can elevate the humble canapé to a work of art. For instance, serving a beet and goat cheese mousse in a delicate endive leaf, topped with microgreens and edible flowers, creates a stunning visual effect. Similarly, presenting sushi-inspired canapés on individual spoons or in miniature bamboo boats adds a touch of elegance and novelty.

Texture is another key element in crafting modern canapés. Combining different textures within a single bite can create a more dynamic and enjoyable eating experience. Consider a canapé that pairs a crispy base with a creamy topping, such as a toasted crostini with whipped feta and roasted cherry tomatoes. The contrast between the crunchy bread and the smooth, tangy cheese creates a delightful balance. Another example is using puff pastry as a base, filled with a rich mushroom duxelles and topped with a crispy fried sage leaf. The interplay of crisp, creamy, and savory elements makes each bite memorable.

Global flavors have also made their way into the world of canapés, reflecting the diverse culinary influences that shape contemporary cuisine. Incorporating spices, herbs, and ingredients from various cultures can add excitement and depth to your canapé offerings. Imagine a bite-sized taco with a spicy black bean filling, topped with avocado crema and a sprinkle of cotija cheese. This Mexican-inspired canapé brings bold flavors and a touch of heat, perfect for adventurous eaters. Similarly, a Thai-inspired canapé might feature a lemongrass and ginger shrimp skewer with a tangy mango dipping sauce, offering a burst of fresh, aromatic flavors.

Dietary considerations are increasingly important in canapé creation. Many guests may have dietary restrictions or preferences, such as gluten-free, dairy-free, or keto diets. Offering a variety of canapés that cater to these needs ensures that all guests can enjoy the spread without worry. For gluten-free options, consider using rice paper, lettuce leaves, or gluten-free crackers as bases. Dairy-free canapés can feature nut-based cheeses or spreads, such as cashew cheese or almond ricotta. Keto-friendly canapés might include ingredients like smoked salmon, avocado, and hard-boiled eggs, which are low in carbohydrates but high in healthy fats.

Sustainability and ethical sourcing are also key considerations for modern canapés. With growing awareness of environmental issues, many hosts and caterers prioritize ingredients that are locally sourced, organic, and ethically produced. This not only supports local farmers and producers but also reduces the carbon footprint associated with transporting food long distances. For example, using locally sourced cheeses, meats, and vegetables can enhance the freshness and flavor of your canapés while supporting the local economy. Additionally, opting for sustainable seafood, such as wild-caught shrimp or farmed mussels, ensures that your canapés are environmentally responsible.

Interactive and DIY elements can add a fun and engaging aspect to canapé service. Allowing guests to customize their canapés according to their preferences can create a more personalized experience. Set up a canapé station with a variety of bases, toppings, and garnishes, and let guests assemble their creations. This could include a bruschetta bar with different types of bread, spreads, and toppings, or a taco station with an array of fillings and salsas. Not only does this encourage interaction and creativity, but it also ensures that guests can tailor their canapés to their dietary needs and taste preferences.

Incorporating unexpected ingredients can also surprise and delight guests. For example, using edible flowers, such as nasturtiums or pansies, can add a pop of color and a subtle floral note to your canapés. Similarly, incorporating unconventional ingredients like seaweed, truffle oil, or exotic fruits can elevate your canapés and introduce guests to new flavors. A canapé featuring seared scallops on a bed of seaweed salad, garnished with a touch of truffle oil, offers a luxurious and unexpected taste experience.

Pairing canapés with complementary beverages can enhance the overall dining experience. Thoughtfully selected wine, beer, or cocktail pairings can highlight the flavors of the canapés and create a harmonious balance. For instance, pairing a spicy tuna tartare canapé with a crisp, refreshing white wine can enhance the flavors and provide a cooling contrast to the heat. Similarly, a rich, savory canapé like a mini beef Wellington might pair well with a robust red wine or a dark, malty beer. When planning your canapé menu, consider consulting with a sommelier or beverage expert to create the perfect pairings.

Finally, attention to detail in preparation and presentation can make all the difference in creating memorable canapés. Ensuring that each canapé is consistently sized and beautifully garnished shows care and professionalism. Using high-quality, sharp knives and proper cutting techniques can result in clean, precise cuts, enhancing the visual appeal. Additionally, serving canapés at the appropriate temperature, whether hot, cold, or room temperature, ensures that they are enjoyed at their best. Paying attention to these details demonstrates a commitment to excellence and elevates the overall canapé experience.

Revamping canapés for modern palates involves a thoughtful blend of fresh ingredients, innovative presentations, and diverse flavors. By incorporating plant-based options, global influences, and considerations for dietary needs, you can create a canapé spread that is both inclusive and exciting. Emphasizing sustainability, interactive elements, and unexpected ingredients can further enhance the appeal of your canapés. With careful attention to detail and a focus on high-quality ingredients, you can craft canapés that are not only visually stunning but also delicious and memorable. One often overlooked but highly impactful aspect of creating modern canapés is the use of innovative plating techniques. Plating is an art form that can transform a simple dish into a visual masterpiece. Consider using geometric shapes, vertical elements, or layered presentations to add dimension and interest to your canapés. For instance, stacking ingredients carefully to create height can make a canapé more visually appealing. A layered smoked salmon and avocado tartare presented in a small glass or a delicate tower of roasted vegetables on a crisp polenta base can captivate guests' attention and evoke a sense of sophistication.

Chapter 4

Main Courses Meat

Beef and Pork: Heritage Recipes Reimagined

Beef and pork have long been staples in culinary traditions worldwide, their rich flavors and versatility making them favorites for a multitude of dishes. As we delve into heritage recipes reimagined, we explore how these classic meats can be transformed with contemporary twists while honoring their storied pasts. This journey through beef and pork will reveal innovative techniques, modern ingredients, and new presentations that breathe fresh life into time-honored favorites.

Beef, often regarded as a cornerstone of Western cuisine, has roots that stretch back centuries. Traditional recipes like beef stew, steak, and roast beef have been cherished for generations. To reimagine these classics, we start with the basics: selecting the right cut of meat. Grass-fed and organic options are preferable, not just for their superior flavor but also for their health benefits and ethical considerations.

Take the classic beef stew, for instance. Traditionally, it's a hearty dish made with chunks of beef, potatoes, carrots, and onions simmered slowly in a rich broth. To reimagine this, consider incorporating global influences. Instead of the usual mirepoix, try adding a sofrito base made with tomatoes, peppers, and garlic, inspired by Spanish cuisine. Replace the standard potatoes with sweet potatoes for a touch of natural sweetness and added nutrition. For the broth, a splash of red wine or a hint of smoked paprika can add depth and complexity.

Steak, another beloved beef dish, can be transformed in myriad ways. While a perfectly grilled ribeye or filet mignon needs little embellishment, the accompaniments and preparation methods offer room for creativity. Imagine a steak marinated in Korean bulgogi sauce, with its blend of soy, garlic, sugar, and sesame, then grilled to perfection and served with kimchi and a side of sticky rice. This fusion of East and West creates a delightful play of flavors and textures, elevating the traditional steak to something truly unique.

For a more subtle reimagining, consider the classic roast beef. Traditionally served with Yorkshire pudding and gravy, this dish can be given a contemporary twist by altering the seasoning and sides. Rub the beef with a mixture of herbs like rosemary, thyme, and lavender for an aromatic crust. Instead of the usual gravy, prepare a red wine reduction with shallots and a touch of balsamic vinegar. Serve with a root vegetable mash, combining parsnips, carrots, and turnips, for a colorful and healthful accompaniment.

Turning to pork, this meat offers an equally rich canvas for reimagined heritage recipes. Pork's versatility allows it to shine in many forms, from succulent roasts to tender chops and flavorful sausages. One classic example is the pork roast. Traditionally seasoned with garlic and herbs, a modern twist could involve a spice rub influenced by Middle Eastern or North African flavors. Think cumin, coriander, and a hint of cinnamon, creating a fragrant and exotic profile. Pair this with a couscous salad featuring dried fruits, nuts, and fresh herbs for a vibrant side dish.

Pork chops, a staple in many households, can also benefit from a contemporary makeover. Instead of the usual breaded and fried preparation, consider a brine to enhance the meat's moisture and flavor. A brine of apple cider, salt, sugar, and spices like cloves and allspice can impart a subtle sweetness and complexity. After brining, sear the chops and finish them in the oven with a glaze of maple syrup and Dijon mustard. Serve with a side of roasted Brussels sprouts and apples for a harmonious blend of flavors.

Sausages, often relegated to simple grilling or frying, can be transformed into gourmet delights with thoughtful preparation and pairing. Imagine making your own sausages with a blend of pork, fennel seeds, garlic, and red wine. Instead of the typical bun, serve these sausages sliced over a bed of creamy polenta with a rich tomato and bell pepper ragu. The combination of textures and flavors elevates the humble sausage to a sophisticated dish worthy of any dinner party.

Another heritage recipe ripe for reimagining is the classic pork belly. Traditionally slow-roasted to achieve a crispy skin and tender meat, pork belly can be given an Asian twist. Marinate the pork belly in a mixture of soy sauce, ginger, garlic, and five-spice powder, then slow-cook it until it's melt-in-your-mouth tender. Finish with a quick blast under the broiler to crisp the skin. Serve with steamed bao buns, pickled vegetables, and hoisin sauce for a modern take on a beloved classic.

In exploring these reimagined beef and pork recipes, it's essential to consider not just the flavors and techniques but also the presentation. Modern plating can transform a rustic dish into a visual feast. Consider using minimalist plating techniques, focusing on clean lines and thoughtful garnishes. A sprinkle of microgreens, a drizzle of reduction, or a dusting of spice can add a touch of elegance to any dish.

Additionally, sustainability and ethical considerations play a crucial role in modern cuisine. Sourcing meat from local, sustainable farms not only supports the community but also ensures higher quality and better flavor. Utilizing the whole animal, a practice known as nose-to-tail cooking, honors the animal and reduces waste. This approach encourages creativity and respect in the kitchen, challenging chefs to create delicious dishes from less commonly used cuts.

Pairing these reimagined dishes with complementary sides and beverages can further enhance the dining experience. Think about how a robust red wine can elevate the flavors of a beef stew or how a crisp apple cider can complement the sweetness of pork. These thoughtful pairings add another layer of sophistication and enjoyment.

The reimagining of heritage recipes for beef and pork is not just about innovation for the sake of it but about honoring the past while embracing the future. It's a celebration of culinary traditions, viewed through the lens of contemporary tastes and techniques. By blending old and new, familiar and exotic, we can create dishes that are both comforting and exciting, paying homage to their roots while offering something fresh and delightful.

In this culinary journey, remember that the essence of cooking lies in experimentation and joy. Don't be afraid to try new ingredients, techniques, and presentations. Let the rich history of beef and pork inspire you, while your creativity leads the way to new, delicious discoveries. Whether you're a seasoned chef or a curious home cook, these reimagined recipes invite you to explore, savor, and celebrate the timeless appeal of beef and pork in new and exciting ways. Exploring the world of beef and pork through heritage recipes reimagined can be a deeply rewarding experience, both for the cook and those enjoying the meal. This journey not only expands your culinary repertoire but also fosters a deeper appreciation for the rich traditions and innovations that shape our food culture.

Poultry with a Progressive Spin

Poultry has been a cornerstone of human diets for centuries, celebrated for its versatility, affordability, and ability to absorb a wide variety of flavors. However, as culinary trends evolve and our palates become more adventurous, there is a growing desire to reimagine traditional poultry dishes with a progressive spin. This new approach to cooking poultry involves incorporating global influences, utilizing modern cooking techniques, and emphasizing health-conscious ingredients without sacrificing flavor or tradition.

Chicken, perhaps the most ubiquitous of all poultry, offers a blank canvas for culinary creativity. One way to breathe new life into classic chicken dishes is by exploring international cuisines. Take the traditional roast chicken, for example. While a perfectly roasted bird with crispy skin and juicy meat is always delightful, adding a marinade inspired by Middle Eastern flavors can transform it into something extraordinary. A mixture of yogurt, garlic, lemon juice, and spices like cumin, coriander, and turmeric can infuse the chicken with a vibrant flavor profile. Marinate the chicken overnight for maximum impact, then roast it to golden perfection. Serve with a side of tabbouleh and a drizzle of tahini sauce for a complete meal.

Another classic chicken dish that benefits from a progressive twist is the humble chicken soup. Traditionally made with a simple broth, vegetables, and chicken, this comfort food can be elevated by introducing elements from Asian cuisine. Consider making a Thai-inspired chicken soup with coconut milk, lemongrass, ginger, and lime leaves. The creamy, aromatic broth pairs beautifully with tender chicken pieces, mushrooms, and baby corn. Garnish with fresh cilantro, chili slices, and a squeeze of lime to brighten the flavors. This version not only warms the soul but also excites the palate with its complex layers of taste.

Turkey, often relegated to holiday feasts, also holds great potential for innovative recipes. One way to modernize turkey is by using ground turkey in place of beef for a lighter, healthier option in familiar dishes. Turkey burgers, for instance, can be reimagined by incorporating Mediterranean ingredients. Mix ground turkey with feta cheese, spinach, garlic, and oregano, then grill to juicy perfection. Serve on a whole-grain bun with a dollop of tzatziki sauce and a side of sweet potato fries for a nutritious and flavorful meal.

Another progressive take on turkey is to prepare it sous-vide. This method involves cooking the turkey in a vacuum-sealed bag at a precise, low temperature in a water bath. The result is a turkey breast that is incredibly moist and tender, with flavors that are deeply infused. For a unique twist, marinate the turkey breast in a mixture of pomegranate molasses, garlic, and fresh herbs before vacuum-sealing and cooking. Once done, quickly sear the turkey in a hot pan to achieve a beautiful, caramelized exterior. Serve with a pomegranate reduction sauce and a side of roasted root vegetables for an elegant and modern presentation.

Duck, with its rich flavor and luxurious texture, is another poultry option that can be reimagined in exciting ways. Traditionally prepared with a focus on its natural fattiness, such as in duck confit, modern techniques can help balance its richness. One approach is to prepare a duck breast with a crisp skin and serve it with a fruit-based sauce that cuts through the fat. A classic pairing is duck with orange, but for a progressive twist, consider using a blackberry and red wine reduction. The tartness of the blackberries complements the richness of the duck, creating a harmonious balance. Serve with a side of wild rice pilaf and sautéed greens for a sophisticated dish that pleases the senses.

Another innovative duck dish is to use it in Asian-inspired recipes. Peking duck is a well-known and beloved preparation, but creating a duck ramen can be equally exciting. Prepare a rich duck broth by simmering duck bones with ginger, garlic, and scallions. Add in pieces of tender duck meat, soft-boiled eggs, and fresh ramen noodles. Garnish with sliced green onions, nori strips, and a sprinkle of sesame seeds. This dish combines the comforting elements of traditional ramen with the luxurious flavor of duck, offering a truly memorable dining experience.

Progressive poultry cooking also means embracing modern dietary trends and health-conscious ingredients. For instance, using air fryers to prepare crispy chicken can significantly reduce the amount of oil needed, resulting in a healthier version of fried chicken. Coat chicken pieces in a mixture of whole-wheat breadcrumbs, paprika, garlic powder, and a touch of cayenne, then air fry until golden and crispy. Serve with a side of coleslaw made with Greek yogurt instead of mayonnaise for a lighter yet satisfying meal.

Incorporating ancient grains like quinoa, farro, and bulgur into poultry dishes is another way to add nutritional value and modern flair. A quinoa-stuffed chicken breast is a great example. Prepare a stuffing mixture with cooked quinoa, sautéed spinach, feta cheese, and sun-dried tomatoes. Butterfly the chicken breasts, stuff with the quinoa mixture, and bake until cooked through. The result is a dish that is not only healthy but also bursting with flavors and textures.

Sustainability is a crucial aspect of modern cooking, and it extends to poultry as well. Choosing free-range, organic, or pasture-raised poultry not only ensures better animal welfare but also often results in superior taste and quality. Additionally, utilizing the whole bird, from the meat to the bones, aligns with a more sustainable and respectful approach to cooking. Making homemade stock from the bones and using every part of the bird reduces waste and enhances the flavor of your dishes.

Pairing these innovative poultry dishes with suitable sides and beverages can further elevate the dining experience. Consider how a crisp, citrusy white wine can enhance the flavors of a lemon-herb roast chicken, or how a bold red wine can complement the richness of a duck dish. Thoughtful pairings add depth and enjoyment to the meal, making it a memorable event.

Incorporating a progressive spin on poultry recipes allows us to honor traditional dishes while embracing new ideas and techniques. It's about finding the balance between the comfort of the familiar and the excitement of the new. Whether you're experimenting with global flavors, modern cooking methods, or health-conscious ingredients, the possibilities are endless. This approach not only enriches your culinary skills but also brings joy and innovation to your table, making every meal a delightful adventure.

As you embark on this journey of reimagining poultry dishes, let your creativity guide you. Explore new ingredients, try different techniques, and most importantly, have fun in the kitchen. The world of poultry is vast and varied, offering endless opportunities to create delicious, progressive meals that honor the past while looking forward to the future. When approaching poultry with a progressive spin, it's also important to consider the role of marinades, rubs, and brines in transforming the flavor and texture of the meat. These elements can introduce a depth of flavor that permeates the poultry, making each bite a delightful experience. For example, a simple brine of water, salt, sugar, and spices like bay leaves, peppercorns, and juniper berries can result in a turkey that is exceptionally moist and flavorful. The process of brining allows the meat to absorb the flavors and retain moisture during cooking, resulting in a more succulent dish.

Game Meat: Tradition Meets Innovation

Game meat, with its deep roots in culinary history and cultural significance, offers a unique opportunity to blend tradition with innovation. From the rustic charm of a venison stew simmering over a fire to the refined elegance of a seared duck breast with a modern twist, game meats can be both nostalgic and forward-thinking. This chapter delves into the rich world of game meats, exploring how traditional recipes can be reimagined with contemporary techniques and flavors to create dishes that are both familiar and exciting.

Venison, one of the most popular game meats, embodies the essence of tradition. Historically, it has been prepared in hearty stews, roasts, and sausages, reflecting the rustic lifestyle of hunters and gatherers.

To honor this tradition while infusing a modern touch, consider preparing a venison loin with a red wine reduction and wild mushroom risotto. Begin by marinating the venison loin in a mixture of red wine, garlic, rosemary, and juniper berries. This not only tenderizes the meat but also imparts a complex, earthy flavor. Sear the marinated loin to develop a rich crust, then finish it in the oven to your preferred doneness. Serve it atop a creamy risotto made with wild mushrooms and a splash of truffle oil. The result is a dish that pays homage to the traditional flavors of the forest while presenting them in a sophisticated, contemporary manner.

Rabbit, another classic game meat, is often associated with rustic French cuisine. Traditionally, rabbit is prepared in a dish known as lapin à la moutarde (rabbit with mustard), where the meat is braised in a creamy mustard sauce. To bring this dish into the modern era, consider deconstructing it and presenting it as a rabbit roulade. Start by deboning the rabbit and spreading a mixture of Dijon mustard, garlic, and fresh herbs over the meat. Roll it up tightly, secure it with kitchen twine, and sear it in a hot pan until golden brown. Finish cooking the roulade in the oven, then slice it into medallions and serve with a mustard cream sauce and a side of roasted root vegetables. This presentation not only elevates the dish but also makes it more approachable for those new to game meats.

Duck, with its rich flavor and luxurious texture, has long been a favorite in both traditional and modern kitchens. One iconic preparation is duck à l'orange, a French classic that pairs the savory meat with a sweet and tangy orange sauce. To modernize this dish, you might prepare a duck breast with a blood orange and pomegranate glaze. Score the skin of the duck breast and season it with salt and pepper. Sear it skin-side down in a hot pan until the skin is crispy and the fat has rendered, then finish it in the oven. For the glaze, reduce freshly squeezed blood orange juice and pomegranate juice with a touch of honey and a splash of balsamic vinegar until it reaches a syrupy consistency. Drizzle the glaze over the sliced duck breast and serve with a side of quinoa salad studded with pomegranate seeds and fresh herbs. This dish retains the essence of the traditional recipe while introducing new flavors and textures that delight the palate.

Wild boar, known for its robust and slightly gamey flavor, is another game meat that offers a wealth of culinary possibilities. Traditionally used in hearty stews and sausages, wild boar can also be an excellent candidate for modern barbecue techniques. Consider preparing wild boar ribs with a spicy fruit glaze. Begin by marinating the ribs in a mixture of apple cider vinegar, garlic, and smoked paprika. Slow-cook the ribs until they are tender, then brush them with a glaze made from apricot preserves, chipotle peppers, and a splash of bourbon. Finish the ribs on the grill to caramelize the glaze and develop a smoky flavor. Serve with a side of coleslaw made with a tangy apple cider vinaigrette. This dish blends the traditional heartiness of wild boar with the bold, contemporary flavors of modern barbecue.

Quail, a small and delicate game bird, has traditionally been roasted or grilled and served whole.

For a modern twist, consider preparing quail stuffed with wild rice and figs. Debone the quail, leaving the legs and wings intact, and stuff it with a mixture of cooked wild rice, chopped dried figs, and toasted nuts. Secure the quail with kitchen twine, sear it in a hot pan, and finish cooking it in the oven. Serve the stuffed quail with a port wine reduction and a side of wilted greens. This preparation not only enhances the flavors of the quail but also offers a visually impressive presentation that is sure to impress your guests.

Pheasant, often associated with festive occasions and elaborate feasts, can also be reimagined with modern cooking techniques. Traditionally, pheasant is roasted or braised, often with a rich sauce. To bring a contemporary touch to this classic bird, consider preparing a sous-vide pheasant breast with a cranberry and red wine sauce. Season the pheasant breast with salt, pepper, and fresh thyme, then vacuum-seal it and cook it sous-vide at a precise temperature to ensure it remains tender and juicy. For the sauce, reduce red wine with fresh cranberries, a touch of honey, and a sprig of rosemary until it thickens. Sear the cooked pheasant breast in a hot pan to develop a golden crust, then slice and serve with the cranberry sauce and a side of roasted Brussels sprouts. This method highlights the delicate flavor of the pheasant while incorporating the tart sweetness of cranberries, resulting in a dish that is both traditional and contemporary.

The key to successfully blending tradition with innovation lies in respecting the inherent qualities of the game meat while exploring new techniques and flavor profiles. By doing so, you can create dishes that honor the past while embracing the future, offering a culinary experience that is both nostalgic and novel. Whether you are preparing a rustic venison stew with a modern twist or a sophisticated duck breast with a contemporary glaze, the possibilities are endless. Embrace the rich history of game meats while allowing your creativity to guide you, and you will discover a world of flavors that is both timeless and exciting.

As you experiment with these recipes, remember that the journey is as important as the destination. Cooking game meat can be a deeply rewarding experience, connecting you to the traditions of the past while allowing you to express your culinary creativity. Don't be afraid to try new techniques, explore unfamiliar ingredients, and most importantly, enjoy the process. The world of game meat is vast and varied, offering endless opportunities to create dishes that are both innovative and deeply rooted in tradition. Exploring the world of game meat also opens doors to sustainable and ethical eating practices. Game animals are typically free-range and wild, resulting in meat that is often leaner and higher in nutrients compared to conventionally raised livestock. This can be a significant factor in creating a more environmentally conscious kitchen. By sourcing game meat from reputable hunters or suppliers who practice sustainable hunting methods, you contribute to the conservation of wildlife habitats and promote biodiversity.

Classic Sauces Revisited

Classic sauces form the backbone of many culinary traditions, serving as the foundation upon which countless dishes are built. These sauces, rooted in history and refined by generations of chefs, each bring a distinct flavor profile and texture to the table. Revisiting these classic sauces not only deepens our appreciation of their origins but also provides opportunities to adapt and innovate.

The five mother sauces, as defined by Auguste Escoffier, are béchamel, velouté, espagnole, hollandaise, and tomato. Each of these sauces can be transformed with modern techniques and flavors while maintaining their classic essence. Let's start with béchamel, the white sauce made from a roux of butter and flour mixed with milk. Traditionally used in dishes like lasagna and moussaka, béchamel can be elevated with subtle tweaks. Infusing the milk with aromatics such as bay leaves, nutmeg, and thyme adds complexity. For a contemporary twist, consider adding roasted garlic or truffle oil to the béchamel, transforming it into a luxurious base for a macaroni and cheese that straddles the line between comfort food and gourmet fare.

Moving on to velouté, another roux-based sauce, but this time with a light stock, such as chicken, fish, or veal. Velouté is often seen as a step towards more complex sauces, like allemande or suprême. To modernize velouté, experiment with different stocks and ingredients. A seafood velouté, enriched with a splash of white wine and finished with a touch of cream, can serve as a sophisticated sauce for poached fish or shellfish. Alternatively, a mushroom velouté, made with a rich mushroom stock and enhanced with a dash of sherry, offers an earthy, umami-rich accompaniment to poultry or pork.

Espagnole, or brown sauce, is a robust and deeply flavored sauce made from a brown roux, veal stock, and tomatoes. It serves as the foundation for many derivative sauces, such as demi-glace and bordelaise. To breathe new life into espagnole, consider incorporating elements from global cuisines. Adding a hint of miso paste can introduce a savory depth, while a splash of port or Madeira wine can elevate the sauce with a touch of sweetness and complexity. Using this updated espagnole as a base, you can create a modern version of a classic dish like beef bourguignon, where the sauce's richness complements the tender, slow-cooked meat.

Hollandaise, a rich and buttery sauce made with egg yolks, lemon juice, and clarified butter, is perhaps best known for its role in eggs Benedict. While hollandaise is typically served with breakfast or brunch dishes, it can be reimagined in various ways. For a lighter, more contemporary take, consider substituting some of the clarified butter with a lighter oil, such as avocado or grapeseed oil. Adding fresh herbs like tarragon or dill can brighten the sauce, making it a perfect accompaniment for grilled fish or steamed vegetables. Alternatively, infusing the hollandaise with citrus zest or even a touch of chili can create a vibrant and zesty sauce that pairs well with a variety of dishes.

The tomato sauce is perhaps the most versatile of the mother sauces, forming the basis for countless dishes across different cuisines. A traditional tomato sauce is made with tomatoes, onions, garlic, and herbs, simmered until thick and flavorful. To modernize this classic, consider roasting the tomatoes and garlic before blending them into the sauce. This method intensifies the flavors, adding a smoky complexity. You can also experiment with different herbs and spices to create unique variations. For instance, adding a touch of smoked paprika and cumin can transform the sauce into a perfect base for shakshuka or a robust topping for grilled meats. Alternatively, incorporating fresh basil and a splash of balsamic vinegar can create a bright and tangy sauce ideal for pasta or bruschetta.

Beyond the mother sauces, there are many classic accompaniments worth revisiting and reinventing. Take, for example, the classic French béarnaise, a derivative of hollandaise made with tarragon, shallots, and vinegar. To give béarnaise a modern twist, you might infuse it with different herbs, such as chervil or cilantro, or add a subtle heat with a pinch of cayenne pepper. This updated béarnaise can be served with a perfectly grilled steak or drizzled over roasted vegetables for a contemporary touch.

Another classic sauce, the Italian pesto, traditionally made with basil, garlic, pine nuts, Parmesan cheese, and olive oil, can be transformed with a variety of ingredients. Consider using arugula or kale in place of basil for a peppery bite, or substitute walnuts or almonds for pine nuts to introduce a different texture and flavor. Adding a squeeze of lemon juice can brighten the sauce, making it a versatile condiment for everything from pasta to grilled chicken to sandwiches.

Sauces from other culinary traditions also offer opportunities for innovation. Consider the classic Spanish romesco, a rich and nutty sauce made from roasted red peppers, tomatoes, almonds, and garlic. To modernize romesco, you might incorporate smoked almonds for an added depth of flavor or add a touch of sherry vinegar for acidity. This updated romesco can serve as a vibrant dip for roasted vegetables, a topping for grilled fish, or a spread for sandwiches.

In revisiting classic sauces, it's also important to consider dietary preferences and restrictions. Many traditional sauces rely on ingredients like butter, cream, and flour, which may not be suitable for all diets. Exploring alternatives can both modernize these sauces and make them accessible to a wider audience. For instance, a vegan béchamel can be made using plant-based milk and a roux of olive oil and flour, resulting in a sauce that retains its creamy texture without the use of dairy. Similarly, a gluten-free velouté can be achieved by using cornstarch or rice flour in place of traditional flour.

Revisiting classic sauces also involves paying attention to the techniques and methods used in their preparation. Embracing modern cooking tools and methods can streamline the process and enhance the results. For example, using an immersion blender can create a smoother, more consistent hollandaise sauce without the risk of the sauce breaking. Similarly, pressure cookers and sous-vide machines can be utilized to develop deeper flavors in sauces like espagnole and tomato sauce, reducing cooking times while preserving the integrity of the ingredients.

The art of sauce-making is a testament to the balance of precision and creativity in cooking. While the foundation of these classic sauces remains rooted in tradition, the potential for innovation is limitless. By experimenting with new ingredients, techniques, and flavor profiles, you can create sauces that honor their origins while appealing to contemporary tastes.

Incorporating these modernized sauces into your cooking repertoire can elevate even the simplest dishes. A well-crafted sauce has the power to transform a meal, adding layers of flavor and complexity that delight the palate. Whether you're preparing a weeknight dinner or a special occasion feast, revisiting classic sauces with a fresh perspective can inspire culinary creativity and ensure that these timeless traditions continue to evolve and thrive. The journey of revisiting classic sauces also brings us to the realm of emulsions and reductions, techniques that have long been used to intensify and balance flavors. Emulsions, like mayonnaise and vinaigrettes, rely on the suspension of one liquid in another. While a traditional mayonnaise is made from egg yolks, oil, and an acid like lemon juice or vinegar, modern variations can include diverse oils, such as avocado or walnut oil, and even the incorporation of unique ingredients like roasted garlic, chipotle, or fresh herbs. These tweaks not only change the flavor profile but also provide opportunities to pair the sauce with a wider variety of dishes.

Modern Sides for Traditional Meats

Pairing traditional meats with modern sides can elevate a meal from good to unforgettable. The contrast between time-honored main dishes and innovative accompaniments creates a delightful dining experience that speaks to both nostalgia and contemporary tastes. Whether you're serving a classic roast beef, succulent pork chops, or a perfectly cooked chicken, the right side dishes can enhance the flavors and create a balanced, memorable meal.

Consider starting with vegetables, which offer endless possibilities for creativity. Roasted vegetables, for instance, can be transformed by incorporating unexpected flavors and textures. Instead of the usual mix of carrots, potatoes, and onions, think about combining root vegetables like parsnips and beets with a drizzle of honey and a sprinkle of za'atar. This Middle Eastern spice blend introduces a new layer of flavor, enhancing the natural sweetness of the vegetables while adding a subtle, aromatic complexity.

For a more vibrant and fresh option, consider a shaved vegetable salad. Using a mandoline, thinly slice a variety of colorful vegetables such as fennel, radishes, and carrots. Toss them with a light vinaigrette made from lemon juice, olive oil, and a touch of Dijon mustard. Top the salad with fresh herbs like dill or mint, and a handful of toasted nuts for added crunch. This light, crisp side dish provides a refreshing contrast to richer meats like roasted lamb or grilled steak.

Grains are another excellent canvas for innovation. A farro salad, for example, can be a hearty and flavorful accompaniment to traditional meats. Cook the farro until it's tender but still has a slight chew, then mix it with roasted cherry tomatoes, sautéed spinach, and crumbled feta cheese. Dress the salad with a simple lemon and olive oil dressing, and finish with a sprinkle of fresh parsley. The nutty flavor of the farro and the tangy feta create a satisfying counterpoint to the savory depth of grilled pork chops or roasted chicken.

Quinoa, often considered a superfood, can be prepared in a myriad of ways to complement traditional meats. For a Mediterranean-inspired side, cook quinoa and mix it with chopped cucumbers, cherry tomatoes, red onions, and Kalamata olives. Add crumbled goat cheese and a dressing made from olive oil, red wine vinegar, and a touch of oregano. This quinoa salad is not only visually appealing but also packed with flavors that pair beautifully with dishes like grilled lamb or baked salmon.

Legumes, too, offer a wealth of possibilities for modern sides. A warm lentil salad, for instance, can be both comforting and sophisticated. Cook green or brown lentils until tender, then toss them with sautéed shallots, garlic, and a splash of balsamic vinegar. Add a handful of fresh arugula and some crumbled blue cheese for a dish that's earthy, tangy, and slightly bitter. This lentil salad pairs wonderfully with robust meats like beef stew or braised short ribs.

Bean salads are another versatile option. For a twist on the classic three-bean salad, use a mix of chickpeas, black beans, and cannellini beans. Toss them with diced bell peppers, red onions, and a cilantro-lime dressing. The bright, zesty flavors of the dressing enhance the creamy texture of the beans, making this salad a perfect side for grilled chicken or barbecued ribs.

Potatoes, a staple side for many traditional meats, can also be reinvented with modern twists. Instead of the usual mashed potatoes, consider a potato and leek gratin. Thinly slice potatoes and leeks, then layer them in a baking dish with a mixture of heavy cream, garlic, and Gruyère cheese. Bake until the top is golden brown and bubbly. This rich and creamy gratin is a luxurious side that complements dishes like roast beef or baked ham.

For a lighter potato dish, try smashed potatoes with herbs. Boil small new potatoes until tender, then gently smash them with the back of a spoon. Drizzle with olive oil, sprinkle with sea salt, and roast until crispy. Finish with a generous handful of chopped fresh herbs like rosemary, thyme, and parsley. These smashed potatoes are crispy on the outside and creamy on the inside, making them a delightful side for grilled steaks or roasted chicken.

Rice dishes can also be updated with contemporary flavors. A coconut rice pilaf, for example, can bring a tropical flair to traditional meats. Cook jasmine rice in a mix of coconut milk and water, then stir in toasted coconut flakes and chopped cilantro. The subtle sweetness and fragrance of the coconut enhance the rice, creating a side dish that pairs well with spicy grilled meats or curry dishes.

For a more robust rice side, consider a wild rice and mushroom pilaf. Cook wild rice until tender, then mix it with sautéed mushrooms, onions, and a splash of white wine. Add fresh thyme and a handful of toasted pecans for a dish that's earthy, nutty, and full of depth. This pilaf is a perfect match for roasted game meats or grilled pork tenderloin.

Salads can also play a key role in modernizing the sides for traditional meats. A kale and apple salad, for instance, combines the hearty texture of kale with the crisp sweetness of apples. Toss chopped kale with thinly sliced apples, toasted walnuts, and a maple-Dijon dressing. The sweet and tangy dressing balances the bitterness of the kale, making this salad a refreshing side for roasted poultry or pork.

Another innovative salad option is a roasted beet and citrus salad. Roast beets until tender, then slice them and arrange with segments of orange and grapefruit. Drizzle with a light vinaigrette made from citrus juice and olive oil, and top with crumbled goat cheese and fresh mint. The vibrant colors and bold flavors of this salad make it a stunning and delicious side for dishes like duck breast or grilled salmon.

Even bread can be reimagined to complement traditional meats. Instead of the usual dinner rolls, consider serving homemade focaccia. Top the focaccia with a mix of caramelized onions, rosemary, and sea salt before baking. The rich, savory flavors of the toppings and the soft, chewy texture of the bread make it a perfect accompaniment for hearty stews or roasted meats.

Cornbread is another classic that can be updated with modern twists. Consider a jalapeño-cheddar cornbread, where the heat of the jalapeños and the sharpness of the cheddar add a new dimension to the traditional recipe. Serve this cornbread with barbecued meats or chili for a side that's both comforting and exciting.

Incorporating modern sides into meals with traditional meats not only enhances the overall dining experience but also allows for creativity and innovation in the kitchen. By experimenting with new flavors, textures, and ingredients, you can create side dishes that not only complement but also elevate the main course. Whether you're hosting a dinner party or preparing a family meal, these modern sides will ensure that your traditional meats are presented in the best possible light, delighting your guests and making every meal memorable. Another inventive approach to modern sides involves exploring the world of fermented and pickled vegetables. These tangy, crisp additions can provide a refreshing counterpoint to rich, savory meats. For example, quick-pickled red onions, made by soaking thinly sliced onions in a mixture of vinegar, water, sugar, and salt, add a bright pop of flavor to grilled steaks or pulled pork sandwiches. Similarly, kimchi, the famous Korean fermented cabbage, offers a spicy, complex taste that pairs excellently with roasted chicken or braised short ribs.